A JOURNEY TO THE WEST

A Journey to the West

BY DOMENICO LAFFI

The Diary of a Seventeenth-
Century Pilgrim from Bologna
to Santiago de Compostela

Translated, with a Commentary

BY JAMES HALL

Published in 1997 by

PRIMAVERA PERS

LEIDEN, THE NETHERLANDS

&

CONSELLERÍA DE CULTURA E COMUNICACIÓN SOCIAL
Xerencia de Promoción do Camiño de Santiago

Photographs

On page 18, 19, 60, 78, 88, 89, 93, 110, 111, 114, 121, 123, 124, 125, 126, 128, 144, 148, 150, 151, 156, 157, 158, 160, 164, 167, 168, 169, 170, 180 and 184 the photographs are by James Hall.

ISBN 90 74310 28 1

ACKNOWLEDGEMENTS

In the course of researching this book we became indebted to very many people for their help and advice. We should first like to thank those correspondents along the pilgrimage road between Bologna and Santiago de Compostela who generously shared their knowledge of the history of their region with us and helped us find illustrations. We were able to meet many of them and enjoy fruitful discussions. In particular we wish to mention the following:

In Italy, Dr Mario Fanti, former director of the Biblioteca Comunale dell'Archiginnasio, Bologna and the present staff of that library; Dr Ernesto Milano, director of the Biblioteca Estense Universitaria, Modena; Comm. Camillo Rossi, director of the Museo della Ghiara, Reggio Emilia; Dr Giovanni Pinna, director of the Museo Civico di Storia Naturale, Milan; Dr Maria Teresa Fiorio, director of the Civiche Raccolte d'Arte and the staff of the Biblioteca Trivulziana, both in the Castello Sforzesco in the same city; Dr Maurizio Cassetti, director of the Archivio di Stato, Vercelli; Dr Marco Carassi, deputy director, Archivio di Stato and Dr Rosanna Roccia, director of the Archivio Storico Comunale, both in Turin; and the Franciscan Missionary Sisters in Assisi.

In France, Mme Esther Moensch, curator of the Musée du Petit Palais, the staff of the Archives Départementales and of the Bibliothèque Municipale, all at Avignon; Pasteur R. Grossi, president of the Société d'Histoire du Protestantisme de Nîmes et du Gard, and Mlle Dominique Darde, curator, and M. Jean Pey of the Musée Archéologique, Nîmes; M. Bernard Jamme, archivist of the church of St-Roch and M. G. Gudin de Vallerin, director of the Médiathèque Gutenberg library, both at Montpellier; the staff of the Archives Municipales at Béziers; M. Yves Solier, curator of the Musée Archéologique and M. Paul-Henri Viala, director of the Archives Municipales, both at Narbonne; Mme Sylvie Caucanas, director of the Archives Départementales de l'Aude at Carcassonne; M. Christian

Cau, director of the Archives Communales de Toulouse, and M. Jean Penent, curator of the Musée Paul Dupuy in the same city; Mlle Anne Marie Denjean, curator of the former abbey of Planselve at Gimont; M. Pierre Debofle, director of the Archives Départementales du Gers, Auch; Me José Barès of Aspet; and M. Jacques Staes, director of the Archives Départementales des Pyrénées-Atlantiques, Pau.

In Spain, D. Emilio Linzoain, archivist and librarian of the Colegiata de Roncesvalles; D. José L. Molins, director of the Archivero del Ayuntamiento de Pamplona and D. Jesús-Maria Omeñaca Sanz, director of the Museo Diocesano in that city; D. José Ignacio Diaz, former editor of Peregrino, Sto Domingo de la Calzada; D. Matias Vicario, director of the Archivo Diocesano, Burgos; D. Antonio Viñayo, abbot of the Colegiata de San Isidoro, León and his staff; DD. Bernardo and Hortensio Velada Graña, the former having been director of the Archivos Diocesano y Capitular at Astorga and D. José Fernandez Pérez, curator of the Museo de los Caminos, also at Astorga; Professor D. Carlos Villanueva, department of the History of Art, University of Santiago de Compostela; D. Alejandro Barral Iglesias, director of the Museo, and D. José-María Díaz, director of the Archivo, Catedral de Santiago; last but by no means least, D. Francisco Singul Lorenzo, art historian of the Dirección Xeral de Promoción del Camino de Santiago, Xunta de Galicia – a very helpful and never-failing source of information in Santiago whose word opened many doors for us.

We should like to thank also Mr James Hogarth and Professor Brian Tate, both of whom very kindly read the book in typescript and made many valuable comments which saved us from pitfalls. To Mr Hogarth we owe, in addition, the translation of Latin passages in the text and the Appendix on Laffi's timetable. We are grateful to our good friend, Pat Quaife, president of the Confraternity of Saint James, whose unrivalled knowledge of people and places along the Camino led us unfailingly to the right person in our search for information.

JAMES & STELLA HALL

Lay-out & typesetting

Cédilles, Amsterdam

CONTENTS

Viaggio in Ponente
A' SAN

GIACOMO

DI GALITIA,
E FINISTERRÆ,

Di D. Domenico Laffi Bolognese;
Aggiuntoui molte curiolità dppo il fuo
terzo Viaggio à quelle Parti.
Con la Tauola de' Capitoli, e cofe più notabili.
TERZA IMPRESSIONE.

All'Illuftriff. e Reuerendiff. Sig. Co:
CARLO EVANGELISTA
GRASSI

Abbate, e Dottore dell'vna, e l'altra Leg-
ge, Preuofto della Metropolitana di San
Pietro, e Confultore della Santiffima
Inquifitione di Bologna.

In Bologna per g'Eredi del Pifarri. 1681.
Con licenza de' Superiori.

ABOUT THE AUTHOR

DOMENICO LAFFI WAS BORN IN 1636 IN A village in the foothills of the Italian Apennines near Bologna. We know almost nothing about his early life, though he tells us he studied at Bologna university. He was ordained into the Church, but instead of settling down to the conventional life of a parish priest he acquired a keen taste for travel. His journeys, mostly made on foot, took him far and wide. He went to Spain four or five times and once to the Holy Land. 'I have no other joy but to travel' he says at the end of this book, in which he describes his journeys to Santiago de Compostela in northwestern Spain.

He was indefatigable. Santiago de Compostela (or Compostella, as it is commonly known in English) is more than thirteen hundred miles from Bologna, yet he went there no less than three times. Moreover, after each visit he was not content to take the shortest way home, but chose instead to make a great detour to the cities of central and southern Spain, once going as far as Córdoba and Granada before heading back to Bologna.

Laffi gives us a lively picture of the conditions of travel in his day. It was one thing to follow the king's highway or the remains of a Roman road. It was quite another to pursue an uncertain track through a forest, or to rely for directions on an occasional stone cairn put up by previous wayfarers. To be overtaken by nightfall in a lonely mountain valley had its dangers. Wolves were sometimes a threat. Rivers presented their own problems: in the absence of a bridge one might face an unscrupulous ferryman or, as a last resort, be obliged to wade across. Laffi once crossed pick-a-back thanks to an obliging companion. There was an ever-present risk of bandits. He heard alarming stories about

A Viaggio in Ponente a San Giacomo di Galitia e Finisterræ, *Bologna, 1673. Revised edition 1681; reprinted 1726, 1738.*

B Viaggio in Levante al Santo Sepolcro di Nostro Signore Giesù Christo et altri luoghi di Terra Santa, *Bologna, 1683.*

C Dalla tomba alla culla è un lungo passo. Viaggio da Padova ove morse il glorioso S. Antonio a Lisbona ove nacque, *Bologna, 1691.*

D *Fantuzzi, Giovanni,* Notizie degli scrittori bolognesi, *vol. 5 of 9 vols. Bologna, 1781-94.*

E *Archives of the church of San Cristoforo, Vedegheto,* Baptizatorum Liber Primus, *vol. 1, p. 13, 1566-1816. Domenico Laffi's play,* L'Ebreo convertito *(1682), is dedicated to the rector of San Cristoforo.*

F *Archivio Generale Arcivescovile, Bologna:* Cancellerie vecchie, *1690, vol. 508, c. 23v.*

G Ibid. *1696, vol. 509. It is also stated here that Domenico Laffi was 64 years old in 1696. He would then have been born in 1632, four years before the date of the baptismal certificate. The latter is presumably correct.*

H *Carrati, Baldassare M.,* Alberi genealogici delle famiglie di Bologna *(end 18th-early 19th century), Biblioteca Comunale dell'Archiginnasio, Bologna (M S Dept.): vol. 14, no. 37; pressmark B. 711.*

them from people he met on the way. He himself was never harmed, though he once had to take to his heels. Food and drink were sometimes scarce in the remoter regions and the weather, especially in the mountains, could be treacherous. He faced all these things, usually calmly, sometimes even with humour.

It is as a writer of travel books that he is remembered. There are three, in which he relates his journey to Compostella,[a] to Jerusalem,[b] and to Lisbon.[c] Jerusalem and Compostella were two of the great centres of pilgrimage in medieval Christendom. Laffi had a special devotion to the latter, where the supposed remains of the apostle, James the son of Zebedee, lay.

It is mainly through his books that we can gain any insights into the man, for independent documents of any kind are rare. 'He enjoyed writing plays and subsequently acquired a taste for travel, to which he devoted the greater part of his life,' says a directory of writers published in 1786.[d] A baptismal certificate exists, dated 3 August, 1636, naming parents and witnesses.[e] According to records compiled at the end of the seventeenth century, when in Bologna he lived in an apartment in the house of the Dolfi family, which was in the parish of St James of the Carbonesi, though he was apparently never priest of that parish.[f] It is also recorded that he devoted himself to teaching Christian doctrine in the church of Santa Maria Inceriola and regularly celebrated Mass at the 'House of the Catechumens'.[g] Surprisingly, his place and date of death are not known for certain though it is supposed he died in Bologna. A tantalizing fragment of a Laffi family tree in the Archiginnasio library of Bologna,[h] includes the following: 'D. Domenico, 1700 Sacerdote e cur.[-ato]'. He would have been 64 or 65 years old in 1700, a likely span of life in that era.

So what do his writings tell us about him? Laffi was a person of educated tastes. On matters of art and architecture he is informative and, on the whole, an accurate guide. His descriptions of buildings and monuments that are no longer standing, or of paintings and sculpture that have since been lost or destroyed, often provide useful information about the past that would otherwise have remained inaccessible to us. He is evidently widely read in Italian and Spanish history and literature, as we can tell from the sources he acknowledges from time to time. His pride in his

i James Hogarth in a letter to the translator.

country's literary heritage is evident in his account (highly questionable) of the death of Petrarch's Laura at Avignon.

Laffi lived in an age of new scientific discoveries and religious controversy that were challenging the Catholic Church's traditional teaching. But he remained true to the old doctrines. For him the earth would always be the centre of the universe, in spite of the alternative claims of his fellow countryman, Galileo. Laffi is at one with the spirit of the Counter-Reformation and deplores what he sees and hears of the activities of Protestants as he travels through southern France. At Nîmes he is surprised to find Catholics and these 'heretics' co-existing amicably. For him every holy relic is genuine. Even the various objects supposed to have belonged to Roland, the hero of Roncesvalles, which he examines with curiosity, seem to him to have a similar aura of sanctity. He is alive to the historic threat to the Christian Church posed by Islam. On his way through Spain, from which the last of the Moorish rulers had been expelled in 1492, he has a ready ear for the legends of epic battles between Christians and Arabs. Indeed, he is sometimes all too ready to assume the literal truth of the more fanciful stories he hears along the way.

Laffi also has his share of human weaknesses, as one commentator has noted: 'His sincerity and piety are not in doubt, but he shows something of a Pepysian frankness in revealing his own feelings and motives. He is happy to accept alms after officiating as a priest, but on another occasion is mortified at being seen to receive alms while in church with gentlemen of his acquaintance; he is ready to join in the celebration of a wedding, worried by the thought that he may have to contribute to the bride's dowry and relieved when she gives him a few coins to pray for her; he welcomes the thought of a free meal, but is disappointed when he finds that he has to pay for it after all; and he confesses to difficulty in restraining his laughter when observing some local custom'.[i]

Laffi went to Compostella in 1666, 1670 and 1673, each time with a travelling companion, though not always the same one. The city had by then been a focus of international Christian pilgrimage for some five hundred years, though the origin of the cult was even earlier. About the year 830 a tomb had been discovered beneath what is now Compostella cathedral, but was then no more than a wooded hill-

A Viaggio in Ponente à San Giacomo di Galitia, e Finisterræ, di D. Domenico Laffi Bolognese. Aggiuntovi molte curiosità doppo il suo terzo Viaggio à quelle Parti. In Bologna per gl'Eredi del Pisarri, 1681. *A useful modern edition is published by the Università degli studi di Perugia, 1989.*

side. It appears to have been a burial chamber dating from the Roman occupation or soon after, and could have been the centre of a local cult, probably Christian. It was claimed, on what are now recognized to be very insecure grounds, that the contents of the tomb were the remains of the apostle, known as James the Greater. A discovery of this importance was bound to have far more than local significance. The cult of the apostle grew steadily until, by the twelfth century, Compostella had become the destination of literally thousands of pilgrims from all over western Christendom. Moreover St James, having been made the patron saint of Spain, also became the spiritual champion of the Christian armies in their struggle to oust the Moors from the peninsula.

Laffi lived in an age when the call to pilgrimage, particularly to more distant shrines, had become less insistent. After the Reformation it had all but ended in the Protestant countries of northern and central Europe. It was also hindered by the Thirty Years' War which, so far as France and Spain were concerned, dragged on until 1659. There had been some falling off, too, as a result of guidelines laid down for pilgrims by the Council of Trent in the mid-sixteenth century, which encouraged them to venerate local shrines in preference to more distant ones. The effect of all this on Italians seems to have been not very significant. Their traditional route to Compostella (via Bologna, Milan, Turin, Montgenèvre, Avignon, Toulouse, Roncesvalles, Pamplona, Burgos and León) was still well trodden. This was Laffi's route. After Compostella he travelled on to Cape Finisterre and the former seaport of Padrón where, according to popular legend, St James' body was miraculously transported by boat after his martyrdom at Jerusalem. Here the present translation ends. At this point Laffi leaves the historic road and makes his way home to Italy by routes that, for the most part, are unrelated to the Compostellan pilgrimage.

The first edition of *A Journey to the West*, covering Laffi's first two visits, was published in Bologna in 1673 and was reprinted three years later. A revised edition, from which the present text is translated,[a] combines the experiences of all three visits and appeared in 1681. It was reprinted four times during the next half century but then remained out of print until the present day.

ABOUT THE AUTHOR

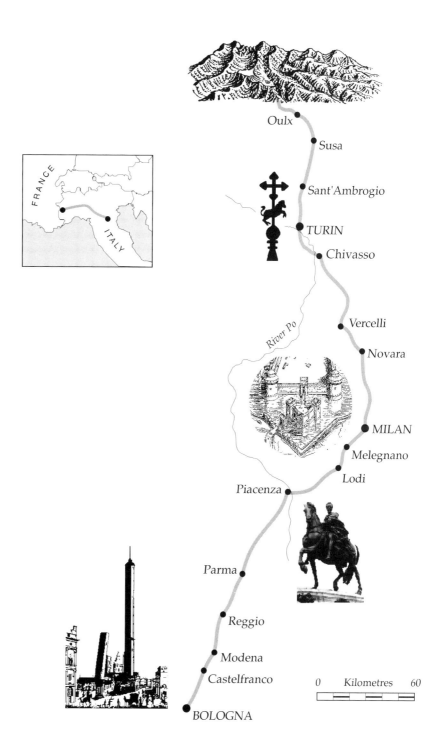

FRANCE

ITALY

Oulx

Susa

Sant'Ambrogio

TURIN

Chivasso

River Po

Vercelli

Novara

MILAN

Melegnano

Lodi

Piacenza

Parma

Reggio

Modena

Castelfranco

BOLOGNA

0   Kilometres   60

13

Fig. 2   *Bologna, the leaning
towers: the Asinelli (1109-19,
97.5 m.), and the Garisenda
(same date, 48 m.). From an
18th-century engraving.*

I

THE AEMILIAN WAY
Bologna to Milan

A *The fortress marked the boundary of one of the States of the Church in that region, which acknowledged papal sovereignty. Most of the fortifications are now in ruins though the principal gatehouse is well preserved. Urban VIII reigned from 1623 to 1644.*

B *'quattrini'.*

C *Italian Renaissance military engineers devised a new type of fortification for besieged cities, known as the bastion system, which was widely adopted in Europe. The bastion, a development of the medieval circular tower, was a four-sided work, projecting from the main rampart. Another typical feature was the ravelin, a diamond-shaped, free-standing outwork protecting a gate into the fortress. It was usually joined to it by a drawbridge. (See fig. 4, p. 16.)*

Laffi usually uses the word demi-lune to denote a ravelin that protects a bastion. Otherwise, it may stand before a rampart midway between two bastions.

YOU WILL DISCOVER, DEAR READER, THAT I have described this journey without any rhetorical flourishes; it is free from elaborate turns of phrase. Such ornate devices would not be appropriate to a pilgrim whose feet are in ceaseless motion, and whose spirit suffers a continual series of minor distractions. I want to describe it in ordinary language so that everyone can understand it.

I, Domenico Laffi and Domenico Codici, a painter, both of us Bolognese, wearing the habit of pilgrims, departed from the city of Bologna on 16 April, 1670, in order to visit the glorious apostle, St James, in Galicia. (Though in the year 1673 I returned to Galicia for the third time in the company of Fra Giuseppe Liparini, a Conventual of the Friars Minor, departing on 8 September.)

We set off towards Modena, passing through Castelfranco, fifteen miles from Bologna. This place is strongly defended, having a fortress with four bastions, and is well supplied with everything needed by a garrison. It was built by the people of Bologna in the time of Pope Urban VIII, and for that reason is known by many as the 'Fort of Urban'. Its purpose was to quell any unexpected attacks or raids by the Modenese.[a]

After passing the fortress you come to a river called the Panaro, which divides the state of Bologna from that of His Serene Highness of Modena. Here you pay thirteen farthings[b] per person in Modenese money. From here to Modena is five miles. When we reached Modena we entered by the gate called the Porta Bolognese, which is fortified with a demi-lune and three drawbridges.[c]

It is a very ancient and noble city. The cathedral is well worth seeing, as much for its antiquity as for the hallowed remains that lie there. There are other good churches, in

A *The House of Este was an ancient*
and famous princely family. The
Duchy of Modena was created in
1452. The new ducal palace, which
was being built when Laffi was
there, was begun in 1634. (It now
houses a military academy.) Be-
sides being on the whole enlight-
ened rulers the Este family were

particular Sant'Agostino, which has been entirely rebuilt. It is painted and decorated with all the saints of the House of Este. It was rebuilt expressly for the funeral of the Most Serene Duke Alfonso d'Este, lately deceased. After that we made our way to the palace of the same Serenissimo. When completed it could be, indeed will be, most magnificent because of the sumptuous marble, which is the very image of regal splendour.

In the old palace, where Their Serene Highnesses now reside, there is, besides the superb appointments and beautiful apartments, a gallery of very famous pictures. In one room the walls are wholly covered with huge mirrors of the finest crystal. They adorn not only the walls but extend over the ceiling – the most striking thing imaginable. In this city there are gentlemen and ladies of noble birth and they hold the most splendid masked balls.[a]

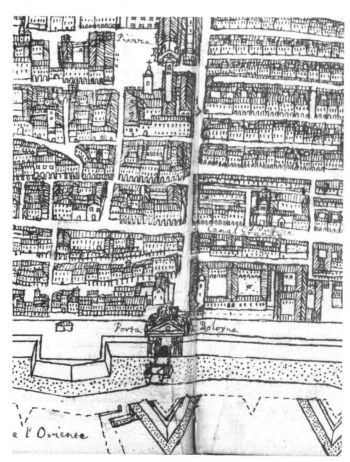

We left by the Sant'Agostino gate, where there is a fort-
collection of paintings and other ress with five 'royal' bastions, built by Duke Francesco. We
works of art, formerly in the old took the road to Reggio, fifteen miles[b] away, crossing a
palace, can now be seen in the great river called the Secchia, where you pay three *soldi*[c]
Galleria Estense, part of the Pa- per head. Beyond the river is a strongly fortified town
lazzo dei Musei. The Romanesque called Rubiera, lying in a plain with water all round it. It
cathedral (begun in 1099, but not belongs to the Serenissimo of Modena. We continued as far
finished until the 13th century) as Reggio, another seven miles from Rubiera.
has a fine west portal. The church
contains the supposed remains This is a very charming and pleasant city, which also be-
of St Geminianus, bishop and longs to the Duke of Modena. Here they make many spurs
patron saint of the city. and fashion large numbers of beautiful objects in bone in a
variety of styles. In the cathedral is the greatly venerated
B 'miglio', approximately an English body of St Prosper, together with other relics and sacred
mile. remains. There are a few excellent churches, in particular
the church of the Madonna of Reggio, whose image, being
so greatly venerated, has been minted on a golden *doppia*.
C A 'soldo' was one twentieth of a The Infant Jesus is in front and the Madonna, with bended
'lira'. knee, is in the act of adoring him. It has the motto: *Quem
genuit, adoravit* [She adored him whom she bore].[d]

From Reggio to Parma is fifteen miles. Here you cross a
D The gold doppia (double) was a bridge, which marks the boundary between Reggio and
coin worth two gold scudi. The Parma. You pay three *soldi*, but monastic orders are exempt,
image was reproduced on medals as are all the citizens of Parma. This is the home of their
and plaquettes as well as on coins. Serene Highnesses, the Farnese. It is a fine city, with strong
It commemorated the power of walls, bastions, demi-lunes, and other exterior fortifica-
the image to protect the citizens of
Reggio from harm, in particular
from an epidemic of the plague
which struck the neighbouring
town of Modena in 1630. Laffi is
not quite right about the motto. It
appears on a silver doppia and on
one- and two-lire pieces. The gold
doppia bears the motto: Aver-
tisti iram indignationis [Thou
turnedst away self-righteous
anger]. See fig. 3, p. 16.

Fig. 5 *The court of the
Palazzo della Pilotta, Parma,
in the 18th century, no longer
standing. (Biblioteca Palatina,
Parma; stampa: Tav.11, DD 38.
Photo: Ernesto Greci.)*

The 'mosaic style' refers to the frescoes in the cupola (c. 1260-70) and the tempera paintings on arches and lunettes. They were mainly executed by Byzantine artists for whom mosaic was the traditional medium, as Laffi recognizes. Both their style and iconography have Byzantine features.

The Farnese were a powerful Italian family whose influence dates from the mid-16th century. Parma became a papal dominion in 1531. In 1534 Alessandro Farnese was elected Pope Paul III and in 1545 made the city over to his natural son Pier Luigi who became the first Duke of Parma. The Duchy of Parma was ruled by the Farnese family for over two centuries. Following the death in 1622 of Ranuccio Farnese (whose equestrian statue can be seen at Piacenza) the dynasty declined. The palace, built between about 1583 and 1622, is still known as the Palazzo della Pilotta. Pilotta, also called 'royal' tennis, is the oldest form of the game from which lawn tennis evolved in the 19th century. The palace was partially destroyed in World War II.

Fig. 6 *Friezes of the church of San Francesco del Prato, Parma (above), and of Parma cathedral (beneath).*

tions. There are many noteworthy things here, in particular the baptistery, a splendid, ancient building in the mosaic style, the main square with its brick paving, and the court in the grounds of His Highness's palace itself, where they play 'pilotta'.[a]

There is a strong, well-fortified citadel, and a fine, broad avenue, beginning at the east gate and leading to the main square. A river runs through the city and has the same name. There are three good bridges over it, which connect one side with the other. There are some very good religious houses and churches, in particular the cathedral, with its superb painting by Correggio in the cupola. There are other fine churches, such as the Observantines', which has

The 'Observantines' church'
would be San Francesco del Prato
(begun in the later 13th century,
completed c. 1400). It has friezes
consisting of a motif somewhat
like an ovolo. There are friezes on
the Romanesque cathedral that
have an interlaced motif, but none
on the Madonna della Steccata
(completed 1539). It is the latter
that has Corinthian capitals. See
fig. 6.

C *Laffi has no further comments on*
the towns he passes through until
he reaches Piacenza, a distance of
38 miles according to his reckon-
ing. Piacenza was the termination
of the Roman road, the Via Aemi-
lia, which Laffi has been follow-
ing since he set out. It was built in
187 B C (beginning at Rimini) by
the consul M. Aemilius Lepidus,
after whom it was named.

ovolo moulding and Corinthian capitals. Then there is the church of the Madonna della Steccata, all gilded, and of the Composite order. It has a double ovolo, interlaced together, and two beautiful doors.[b]

His Highness's palace is a very grand and splendid edifice, but is as yet unfinished, so one could say it is an artistic 'endeavour'. There is a College of Chivalry so big that it can accommodate two hundred or more members. It is administered by the reverend fathers of the Society of Jesus. Here they teach every kind of knowledge and all the principles of chivalry, under the patronage of His Highness. [...][c]

Fig. 7 *Alessandro Farnese,*
equestrian statue in the Piazza
Cavalli, Piacenza, by Fran-
cesco Mochi, 1625.

A *The citadel founded by Alessandro Farnese (who was an authority on military architecture) is at Parma!*

B *The bronze equestrian statues represent Ranuccio Farnese and his father Alessandro (1545-92), known as the 'Prince of Parma'. They were done in 1620 and 1625 respectively, by the Tuscan sculptor Francesco Mochi and are in a typically exuberant Baroque style. See fig. 7, p. 19.*

This city [Piacenza] belongs to the Duke of Parma. It is a fine place and has a strong citadel, which was founded by Duke Alessandro Farnese.[a] It is a noble place and does much trade, being greatly helped by the Po, which runs close to its walls. It has an abundance of everything needed for human subsistence. In the main square are two great pedestals, on top of which stand two famous horses carrying on their backs the statues of two dukes. They are all in bronze and are works of great value.[b] In the church of Santo Spirito lies the body of San Fabiano, as well as many other relics. These I omit entirely, in order not to weary the reader – for we must resume our journey, still having a great distance to go.

After crossing the Po, where members of religious orders may pass without paying anything, we came to Zorlesco, twelve miles from Piacenza. From here to Lodi is ten miles, but in order to shorten our journey we walked round inside the walls where we were able to see the splendid fortifications, and many other remarkable things. From Lodi to Melegnano is ten miles, and from there to Milan another ten.

2

THE EIGHTH WONDER
& OTHER MARVELS
Milan to Turin

A *A patent, in the general sense, is an official document that confers an exclusive right upon its owner. The patent mentioned by Laffi is the so-called 'dimissory' letter which, having been signed by a bishop or other prelate, authorized him to celebrate Mass in a diocese other than his own.*

B *The palace is largely the same as in Laffi's day. The courtyards are the work of the architect, sculptor and painter, Tibaldi (1570). Some alterations were made at the end of the 18th century. The underground passage still exists and is used by canons of the cathedral. The braccio was usually 55 cm., but varied from one district to another. It measured about 60 cm. in Bologna and 68 cm. in Milan. Laffi's measurements cannot always be trusted.*

C *At Halicarnassus.*

D *At Ephesus.*

E *The Visconti, a powerful Lombard family, ruled Milan for nearly two centuries. Gian Galeazzo (d. 1402), who was created Duke of Milan in 1395, was an unscrupulous tyrant who had hopes of ruling the whole of the Italian*

W E ENTERED MILAN BY THE PORTA ROMana and, once inside the city, continued as far as the Porta Vigentina. Here we turned to the right and found a good hostelry where we lodged for a few days. By then it was evening, so we did not go round the city, but next morning we went to the archbishop's palace to have our patents signed, so that we could celebrate Mass.[a]

The palace surpasses all others in size, beauty and antiquity, and is therefore well worth seeing. It is counted among the most splendid of archiepiscopal palaces in the whole of Christendom. It stands by itself and is in the shape of a square, though not exactly so, since the principal facade, which faces east, and the other that corresponds to it, are 210 *braccia* wide, while the lateral ones are 180 *br*. The total length all round is therefore 780 *br*. There are two courtyards, each with fine facades and arcades going round them, and there are countless rooms and a splendid and spacious reception hall. Below, there is a truly noble underground passage-way leading to the cathedral. It is 40 *br.* long and four wide.[b]

From here we went to the cathedral, which may, justifiably, be counted among the Wonders of the World. Of all the supreme works of man which exist in the world today, or which used to exist, ancient writers designated seven, which they called Wonders, because they seemed to exceed human capability. These were the Colossus of Rhodes, the great wall of Babylon, the pyramids of Egypt, the mausoleum of Artemisia,[c] the temple of Diana,[d] the statue of Jupiter at Olympia, and the hanging gardens at Babylon, which were contrived with great skill above arches and huge towers. This cathedral should, I declare, be the Eighth. It was begun by Gian Galeazzo Visconti,[e] Duke of

tion of his grandiose ambitions.
Its dimensions are exceeded only
by St Peter's, Rome. While the
overall plan, which was the work
of German architects collaborat-
ing with Italian engineers, is gen-
erally admired, the extravagances
of its late Gothic ornament are
not to everyone's taste today.

A *Including the central nave.*

B *Completed by Napoleon in 1813.*

C *Laffi, clearly overwhelmed by*
the splendour of the building, de-
scribes the cathedral in painstak-
ing detail. He gives measurements
of all the main architectural fea-
tures including length and circum-
ference of columns, dimensions
of windows and even the organ.
These and some other rather con-
fusing details I have omitted.
(Laffi's source was Muriggi, F. Pào-
lo, Il Duomo di Milano.)

D *St Ambrose (?340-97) was one of*
the four western Fathers of the
Church. He was bishop of Milan
at a time when the city was an im-
portant administrative centre of
the western Roman Empire. Pagan
religions were still a force to be
reckoned with by the Church. This
often brought Ambrose into con-
flict with the secular authorities.
The best known – widely depicted
in Christian art – is the scene
showing him on the steps of a
church compelling the Emperor
Theodosius I to do public pen-
ance for a particularly cruel
offence.

E *The veneration of sacred relics was*
widespread by the fourth century.
The remains of early Christian

Milan, in 1386. It is built entirely of white marble inside and out and is in the form of a cross. This great church has five aisles.[a] They begin at the facade, which is not yet finished,[b] where there will be five doors. It has four series of carved figures. The bell-tower has two fine stairways. As I said, everything is of white marble. [...][c]

In the interior there are forty-two great windows of stained glass, all of them depicting beautiful stories with human figures. There are three larger windows in the choir, and there will be three more in the facade, all depicting stories from the Old and New Testaments. All the altars have splendid ironwork grilles and their steps are of variegated marbles. The choir is superb. It is difficult to describe, because even the smallest part of it is of such excellent workmanship and materials. But I shall do the best I can. To begin with, the organ is miraculously crafted. There are seventy-two choir stalls of inlaid walnut, on which are seventy-two stories from the life of St Ambrose.[d] They are all done in inlay with ornaments and splendid figures in *mezzo-rilievo*.

I shall leave aside the stairs, balustrades, choir stalls, pulpits, organs, tabernacles, the surroundings that frame the three sanctuaries – that is, the mouldings – the retables and pediments, the fonts, confessionals, and the things required for Mass. The stained glass of the great windows is beyond price. Then there are wonderful tombs of the archbishops, but to describe their beauty and their style of architecture would take too long. There are many holy relics and other sacred remains here but, lest I weary the reader, I shall describe only a few. First, there is the sacred nail, which was given to St Ambrose by the Emperor Theodosius. Under the high altar lie eleven bodies of the Holy Innocents, and twenty-one other sacred bodies, complete with their names – which I omit for the sake of brevity. There are also countless relics of Our Lord, Our Lady, the holy apostles and prophets, the holy martyrs, bishops, confessors, virgins, and innumerable others. If I were to describe them individually it would fill a thick volume.[e]

But I must mention St Charles Borromeo, who lies under the cathedral in a separate chapel, where we went to celebrate Mass. This chapel is situated approximately below the choir and there reposes the body of St Charles in a glass coffin that has figures carved on it of fine craftsmanship.

martyrs, together with their per-
sonal possessions, were carefully
preserved in the belief that some
of the beneficent influence of
the living person was passed on
through them. The Council of
Trent in the sixteenth century
gave a new stimulus to the cult of
relics. The sacred nail, supposedly
used to crucify Christ, is only one
of some twenty scattered through-
out Christendom.

F *Charles Borromeo (1538-84)*
became a cardinal at the age of
twenty-two and archbishop of
Milan four years later. He was a
vigorous, sometimes unpopular,
reformer, but personally selfless
and a friend of the sick and needy.
He is especially remembered for
ministering to the victims of the
plague in Milan in 1576, a subject
widely depicted in Italian Ba-
roque painting. Laffi's reference
to Mass being celebrated accord-
ing to the Roman rite only in
St Charles's chapel alludes to the
use of a different, non-Roman
rite, the 'Ambrosian', that was
customary elsewhere in the Milan
diocese.

G *The Church of Rome was thus*
designated by St Peter.

H *Nephew of St Charles.*

The glorious body rests in the coffin, supine, and is dressed in archbishop's vestments, with inquisitor's stole, mitre and pastoral staff. It should be seen by everyone both out of devotion and because of its beauty. Mass is celebrated according to the Roman rite in this chapel only.[f]

I shall not describe the indulgences that are granted in great numbers by this cathedral, nor the high offices, nor those who occupy them. But I should mention that there is a great quantity of metal craft objects in use, such as altar-crosses of silver, gold, bronze and crystal; candelabra, pax-boards, chalices, and bowls with their little bronze figures, and other vessels of the same material. There are silver tabernacles and lamps, and richly decorated hangings for the altars which are magnificent to behold. This church was appointed by the holy apostle Barnabas to be the head and metropolitan of all the churches of the West, after Rome.[g] It was granted many privileges which are still enjoyed by its archbishops. There are, moreover, a large number of monasteries, colleges, and charitable houses.

Then there is the Ambrosian Library, which deserves to be seen by everyone. It was founded on 8 September, 1607, by Cardinal Federico Borromeo.[h] To administer it he chose nine young scholars, who made it their sole concern. They were well versed in various branches of learning, including languages. Latterly they are translating into Italian and Latin books of divers languages, such as Greek, Arabic, Hebrew, Chaldaean and Persian. For this purpose they have brought in scholars from those eastern countries. They have come to study and then to translate these languages and, ultimately to learn how to teach them. They are drawn not only from the East, but from the whole world. So, they study all kinds of languages here, ones that are today found throughout the world, such as Syriac, Armenian and Abyssinian.

These young men of whom I speak are continually at their studies. Every day they are translating all sorts of languages. Then they pass on their learning to others who follow after them in the library and who themselves become adept in such languages, having been so well taught. Moreover, to further their objectives they send men, well versed in literature, to every corner of the globe to buy many different kinds of books. They bring back a large number of costly and valuable books of great variety, not only books,

C *The Castello Sforzesco is named after Francesco Sforza (1401-66), who had it built. He was a condottiere of peasant stock who rose to become Duke of Milan (in succession to the Visconti). He was a powerful and ruthless ruler. The castle was begun in 1455 on the site of a previous (14th century) stronghold. It was restored three times: first, in 1521 after an explosion that destroyed the Filarete Tower (rebuilt in accordance with the design of the architect after whom it is named); again in 1893-1904 after long use as a barracks; lastly in 1943 when it was badly*

but prints and manuscripts, whole chests full of them. These young men are always studying here. If anyone wants to see a book, they will provide it. They also provide you with paper, pen and ink, and a chair to sit on. In other words they supply everything you might need for the purpose. Moreover they are very well paid and have their own apartments adjoining the library.[a]

No one should be surprised if I linger somewhat over describing the things of Milan because, before I went, besides reading the books mentioned just now, I was personally acquainted with many Milanese gentlemen. In particular, with Signori Giacomo Filippo Pizzali, Carl'Antonio Giordani and Bartolomeo Biondi, all of whom are my patrons and friends. And there are many others whom I must omit, for the sake of brevity.

Next, I went to see the church of Sant'Ambrogio where the bodies of Saints Gervase and Protase lie. In the church of the Franciscan Conventuals are the bodies of Saints Nabor and Felix. The body of St Peter Martyr is in the church of Sant'Eustorgio, of the Order of Preachers. For the sake of brevity I have to leave out very many monasteries and fine churches, hallowed by many sacred bodies and relics, and requiring large reliquaries.[b]

For the remainder of our stay we went to see Sig. Antonio Lucino, whom we had earlier called on in Bologna at the College of Chivalry of St Francis Xavier. He kindly showed us round his palace hung with numerous paintings of famous men. He showed us many courtesies, and provided us with refreshment. Not only that, but he sent us in a coach, accompanied by a groom and a major-domo to see many of the remarkable sights to be found in Milan. First, we saw the splendid and well-fortified castle,[c] which stands in one quarter of the great city. I say great because, except for Rome, it is the largest and most powerful city in Italy. The castle is surrounded by a wall with bastions evenly spaced one from the next. It has a moat full of water, which goes right round so that its two ends meet. This very strong castle, having been constructed according to all the rules of fortification, is reckoned to be impregnable.

At the entrance to the castle, at the first bridge, we passed many guards on both sides. There are many portcullises, gatehouses with an inner portcullis and drawbridges. When we reached the first courtyard we were assigned to a

bombed, with the loss of many archives and other treasures. Today none of the outworks remain. The square, central fortress and its bastions still stand. The ditches are dry.

It appears Laffi must have entered by way of the ravelin that protected the south-east facade (in the foreground of the illustration).

D *A* place d'armes *was an area where troops assembled and the area inside a ravelin was commonly used for this purpose. It is here that one would expect to find the soldiers' quarters, as he confirms. (Today it is the main square that is known, less appropriately, as a* place d'armes.)

E *The 'great archway' would be the Filarete Tower, leading to the main square. The 'inner moat' lies at the far end of this square.*

corporal who was accompanied by a soldier with a great bunch of keys. He led us across the courtyard, which is very big indeed and is used as a *place d'armes.*[d] The soldiers' quarters are here, and are well laid out. There is one enormous piece of artillery. Next, we passed under a great archway,[e] which has a door and a portcullis, and leads to the main square of the castle. Before the arch – or, one should call it, the great gateway – there are two cannons, the biggest

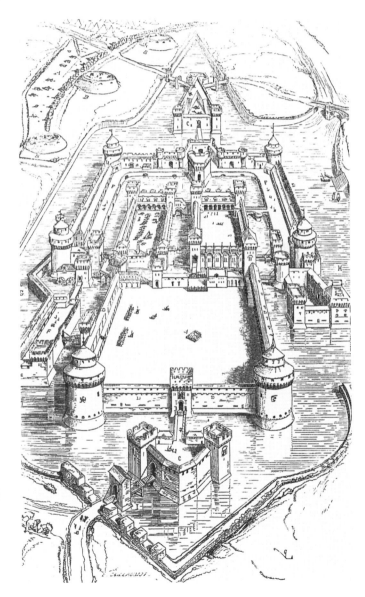

Fig. 8 *Castello Sforzesco, Milan, as it was in the early 16th century. (From a drawing by E.Viollet-le-Duc.)*

It seems that none of the towers ever had a sloping way that took carriages, though the round bastions at each corner of the southeast facade have circular flights of steps leading up to the covered ways. No artillery remains and I have been unable to verify the following story about the soldier's reprieve from his death sentence.

Fig. 9 *'Schiavo inca-tenato', the Enchained Slave. (Museo Civico di Storia Naturale, Milan.)*

I have seen in all my days. Next, we went through another huge gatehouse, also with a portcullis, and crossed over the inner moat. We climbed the main towers, going round and round up a sloping way that takes carriages.[a] At the top, all round the four walls, there are countless pieces of artillery, large and small. Inside the two greater towers are the largest pieces.

On coming out, we saw a cannon, from which a piece about a span's length had been cut from the end of the barrel. It has a commemorative inscription on it, which tells how a soldier, condemned to death, pleaded with the city governor to grant him one favour: that before he died he might be allowed to fire a cannon, but in such a way that no one would be harmed. Consent was given. The soldier mounted the wall and aimed the gun, having already loaded it. He promised he would make a direct hit on the head of a bronze statue that stood on the top of a bell-tower, so far away that is was barely visible. He fired and, to the governor's astonishment, the cannon ball severed the head from the body of the statue. In admiration for such marvellous marksmanship, and in order not to lose this dauntless soldier, the governor pardoned him. He had the end of the gun barrel cut off and engraved, as I said, in commemoration.

Afterwards, we walked round the parapets from where you can see for a great distance on all sides. The external and internal fortifications are very impressive, as are the quarters of the artillery men, the parade ground, and the store rooms for victualling and ammunition. Round the outside of the castle there are six bastions, each having twelve large pieces of artillery. Each of the curtain walls has six cannons and many mortars. The latter are two *braccia* in length, but are broad and thick. At the top of the bastions are turrets where sentries are posted. The bastions have orillons with gun emplacements, the moat has a drainage ditch, there are ravelins, a walled counterscarp with a covered way along the top of it, and other well-constructed fortifications – which I omit for the sake of brevity.

After seeing all this we visited the famous and very magnificent hospital. It is so big it has a room for two thousand sick men and women. From here we went to San Celso, a very beautiful church built of the finest marble with capitals and bases all of bronze, both outside and in. On leav-

B *The museum created by Manfredo Settala (1600-80) was in its day one of the most important cultural institutions in Milan and was internationally famous. It was housed in the family residence, the Palazzo Settala, which today is 26, via Pantano. In 1751 the collection was handed over to the Ambrosian Library and divided up. It suffered many losses, some through neglect of the more perishable items, even more from Napoleon's depredations during his Italian campaign and, most seriously, from allied bombing in the Second World War, Only a small part of the original collection remains today. It is shared between the Civic Museum of Natural History, the Ambrosian Library and the Civic Collections of Applied Art, all in Milan.*

Settala devoted the last fifty years of his life to assembling his museum. He was a man of eclectic tastes, as the richness and variety of his collection demonstrates. He had a strong scientific bent and was also a craftsman and technician. The optical devices and other scientific instruments, not to mention mechanical toys, were mostly made by him in a workshop he set up near the church of S. Nazaro Maggiore (where he was canon). Best known were his burning-glasses, mentioned by Laffi. It was said they could set fire to a wooden plank at a distance of seven metres taking no longer than the time needed 'to say an Ave Maria'.

The 'Satyr' that so alarmed Laffi is preserved intact in the Natural History Museum. It is known as the Schiavo incatenato, the Enchained Slave. The mechanism of

ing there we went to see the governor's palace. Here, they were making fifteen magnificent coaches and the same number of two-wheeled carriages, gilded and wrought with various figurative designs, all done by the most skilled craftsmen. They were to be used at the installation of the new governor, the Duke of Ossona. Apart from them, they were also making many other remarkable things.

We continued onwards and went to see the wonderful studio – or rather gallery – of Canon Manfredo Settala.[b] Here you can see some very curious objects. He has made mirrors of steel which, by reflecting the light, will cause any kind of material to melt immediately, no matter how hard it may be. They can also kindle fire. There are many kinds of perpetual motion machines. Two of them are built like towers, two *braccia* high. If you put a ball of bronze, or some other metal, at the top it runs down a spiral channel. On reaching the bottom it enters a little doorway in the tower, where some mechanical contrivance inside causes it to rise to the top again. Here it emerges through a little window, and returns once more to the bottom in the same manner. The other tower has almost the same movement, except that the channel is arranged differently. Also, the manner in which it goes to the bottom, enters the door and is made to rise to the top again works differently.

Then there is another kind of pillar, the height of a man, the outside all decorated with wood-carvings. It has a tiny glass peep-hole, so that you can look inside to satisfy your curiosity about what is concealed within, quite close to the eye. Lo and behold, a shutter suddenly drops from the front of the glass, and there before you is a Satyr, life-size. It leaps forward in a great bound, stretching out its arms as if to seize whoever is there. It opens its mouth, rolls its eyes and, tossing its head, emits a great bellow. Then it shakes the chains that bind it, as if summoning the strength to break out. This causes no little alarm to anyone who has not previously been warned about it.[c]

Among other things there are very good reproductions of dogs, cats and mice, all done to scale, arranged one behind the other and all made with great skill. Then there are ores from all sorts of mines, such as those from which they extract gold, silver, copper, iron and lead, and all other kind of metal. There are ores of yet another kind from which they obtain a variety of precious stones, such as dia-

this ingenious automaton was set in motion simply by the weight of the unsuspecting visitor when he stood before it. See fig. 9, p. 26.

monds, rubies and so on, and there are all kinds of coral. Then there are medals of gold, silver, bronze, brass and other metal, engraved with representations of the world's famous men, such as emperors, kings, dukes, princes and others, who were remarkable for their piety or tyranny, or some other singular virtue or notorious vice.

You can see a most skilfully constructed organ that consists of a single pipe. It can produce all the sounds that are possible for any other type of organ. The pipe is made with more holes, rods, springs and other mechanical devices than I would know how to describe. I can only say that the more I looked at it, the more I admired its amazing craftsmanship. It must have cost the canon many a long year. Among all these remarkable curiosities the following are also worth seeing: first, there is a large carved kind of pepper-corn with all thirty-two chess-men inside it. There is a kind of cherry stone, made of ivory and of natural size, that has one hundred death's heads engraved on it, and inside it, too, is a complete set of chess-men. Then there are three boxes, each one of them containing another twenty-four, one within the other, each one being successively smaller and more tightly fitting, so that the smallest could scarcely contain a flea. There are coaches drawn by four horses, with ladies inside and a coachman standing up. They are so small a bee's wing would cover them.

You may also see here a block of stone, one *braccio* in length, on which is a realistic representation of a city with a high tower, thought to be Bologna. There is also a red marble ball carved with an image of Our Lady, done in the customary way of artists. There is another similar ball with a death's head on it, so well and so cunningly portrayed. Yet again, you can see another stone whose powder, when deposited in the bark of a oak tree and wetted by the rain, will generate fungi. You can see a coach with four horses, different from the above because it has huntsmen and dogs. It is made of ivory and small enough to go through the eye of a needle. There is an ivory camel, and, below, four armed men fighting one another – and the whole thing would go through the eye of a needle.

Finally, there are two crucifixes, with the Blessed Virgin and St John the Evangelist. One is of ivory, the other of brass, and both would go through the eye of an ordinary needle. There are also two other crucifixes, with the two

A *Laffi refers to Terzago, P.M. (whom he calls Tergasti),* Musæum septalianum..., *Tortona, 1664. This Latin work was translated into Italian by Scarabelli, P.F.,* Museo ò Galeria adunata dal sapere, e dallo studio del Sig. Canonico Manfredo Settala, *Tortona, 1666.*

B *Today Porta Magenta.*

thieves at the sides and, below, the Blessed Virgin, Mary Magdalene, St John weeping, and Longinus on horseback, with his lance resting against the side of the Lord. Between the crosses one can see the city of Jerusalem. All these works are no bigger than one's little finger nail – in short, so small they would serve as a gemstone on a ring. To describe the countless other things to you would fill a large book – indeed they are already in the thick volumes of Terzago and Scarabelli,[a] to whom I would therefore refer the inquiring reader.

We returned to our hostelry, which was near at hand, and sent the coach back to the canon. Next morning we went to thank him and take our leave. Once more we were overcome by his kindness as he plied us with refreshment. On our departure he further earned our gratitude by handing us some doubloons issued by a banker in Madrid. So we left, having received many courtesies inspired by his innate kindness. We left the city by the Porta Vercellina,[b] where they searched our wallets but found no contraband. We then made our way to Rosate, twelve miles from Milan, then to Boffalora sul Ticino, another seven miles, and thence to the city of Novara, sixteen miles from Boffalora.

This city is the last one in the province, or rather the state of Milan, before one enters the province of Piedmont. It is very well protected. There is a large garrison which keeps a sharp eye open because of the very suspect affairs that go on here, it being a frontier town. When we arrived at the gate we were questioned by the first sentry as to our surnames, forenames and country of birth. He then let us enter the gate where the guard-room was situated. Here we were asked the same questions by an officer, who then ordered a soldier to conduct us into the city. We were taken before the Major who asked the same questions that had been put to us at the gate. After receiving his permission we went to a hostelry. Here we met a Frenchman whom we joined up with. He was on his way to Turin and was armed only with a sword. Early next morning we resumed our journey. It was raining a little when we set out, but it got much heavier as we covered the fifteen miles from Novara to Vercelli. We had to cross many rivers, either by boat or by wading through, before we reached Vercelli.

Vercelli is a town in the province of Piedmont, and belongs to the Duke of Savoy. The fortifications are excellent

The fausse-braye *was a low, outer rampart, topped by a parapet, situated outside the moat or ditch. It gave defenders command of the ditch.*

and all newly built. It has walls, and bastions with lead-roofed turrets that look very fine. There is a *fausse-braye* all round, a moat and a secondary moat with two demi-lunes, ravelins and covered ways with benches and parapets.[a]

It is all faced with brick on the outside, which is very costly but gives strength. The gatehouse by which we entered lies to the east, towards Novara. There is certainly no other like it in Italy. I say this not so much because of its architecture and masonry, but because of its size. It is an extraordinary structure, like a veritable palace. Over the archway of the gatehouse are rooms and a hall so large that it can hold four hundred soldiers. It has some very fine iron railings on the inside and outside, well worth seeing. The other gate which goes towards Turin is also very unusual. Though it is smaller it is of very pleasing architecture and most excellent stone-work. Being a frontier town, it has a large garrison stationed in it. On entering, we took a look round the town. It is very pleasant, though not big. There are many religious houses of both nuns and friars. In the Dominican monastery is a belt, the so-called 'chastity belt' with which angels girded St Thomas Aquinas when he was

Fig. 10 *The 17th-century gatehouse to the east of Vercelli. Its garrison was accommodated in the upper rooms.*

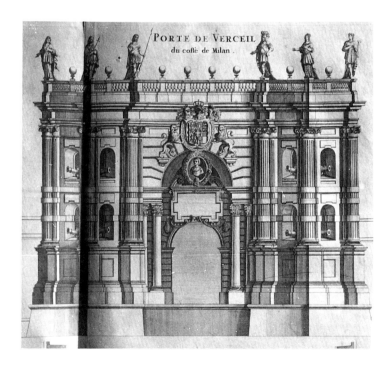

held prisoner at Roccasecca. From that time he lived in perpetual chastity.[b]

On leaving we set off towards San Germano, twelve miles away. At the gate they wanted, yet again, to see inside our wallets before letting us go. We spent the night at San Germano, and a very bad one it was as regards sleeping and eating because, in the small hostelries such as they were, there was nothing to be had. After that we went through many stretches of open countryside until we arrived at a place called Il Bosco.[c] It had been a fortified town but was completely laid waste as a result of the wars. It was pitiful to see the ruined palaces, houses and churches where trees had grown up among them, transforming the place into a wood. Outside the gate, which stood in total ruins, there was a mill, where we betook ourselves, driven by hunger. Here we came upon a peasant in the company of the miller, who were having a meal. After we had pleaded with them for a long time, they have us a little bread and cheese (which must have been made in the age of Romulus and Remus) and a little wine which, from being near the water, had become its sworn companion.

From here we went to Chivasso, another ten miles. We arrived in the evening, having seen Bodia on the way, a walled town that has little to commend it. We were well looked after, both as to victuals and sleeping arrangements. The place is well protected with external fortifications. And they make a good aqua-vitae. In the morning we headed towards Turin. There had been a great deluge of rain over the region, flooding everything, so that we were unable to distinguish the roads from the fields. We crossed the Po by boat, opposite Chivasso. It was very dangerous because the river was swollen by the rains, and we were driven backwards two or three times, the boat nearly overturning. But with the help of God and St James the Apostle, we crossed over. Then we followed the bank of the Po through wooded country, for fifteen miles to Turin.

Fig. 11   *Civic Tower, Turin.*
(Engraved from a drawing by
Tommaso Borgonio, 1665-6.
Archivio Storico, Turin.)

3

THE WINDING-SHEET OF GOD

Turin to the Dauphiné

A *The 'great bridge' that Laffi crossed to enter the city would have been the Ponte di Po, today the Ponte Vittorio Emanuele 1. In his day it was the only way into the city from the other side of the river. It was rebuilt by Napoleon. The 'broad thoroughfare' was the present-day Via Po. His Royal Highness was Carlo Emanuele 1 (1580-1630), Duke of Savoy, who undertook a great reconstruction and enlargement of the city. The House of Savoy, known as the 'gatekeeper of the Alps', formed a powerful and independent duchy until the early nineteenth century. Its capital was Turin.*

B *The square which Laffi calls the royal piazza is in fact the Piazza Castello. In his day the square known as the 'royal piazza' was what is now called the San Carlo. The arcade connected the Palazzo Madama in the centre of the square with the ducal palace on the north side and porticoed buildings on the south. Its decorative scheme was typically baroque, comprising ceiling paintings as well as the statuary mentioned by Laffi. It was described by the Italian painter, Federico Zuccaro, who supervised the work: 'The great arcade will be a compendium of*

O N R E A C H I N G T U R I N W E C R O S S E D A G R E A T bridge over the Po. In the middle is a drawbridge which they raise at night on the city side, leaving a gap in the bridge. We kept straight on along a new, broad thoroughfare where, every day, they are building churches, palaces and houses, His Royal Highness having enlarged the city by encircling it with a wall. We entered by the gate called the Po and came to the first portcullis.[a] The guard asked us to what town we belonged, which way we had come, and where we were going. We told him we were Bolognese and were going to Galicia. Once more we were asked for passports and health certificates, and after they had been examined we were allowed in. Having passed all the sentries and portcullises we came to the royal piazza, which is square and surrounded by splendid mansions. On the far side is the royal palace. A magnificent arcade runs through the middle of the square from one side to the other. It is crowded with statues up to the ceiling, and is supported by fine columns.[b] The royal guards stand under it. Then there are two huge cannons and a great bronze mortar that fires bombs. Out of curiosity, I measured it. It is 30 spans in length, 12 wide, and weighs 10,596 pounds.

From here we went to the cathedral where we sought absolution at the high altar. High above it is the Holy Shroud, in which the body of Christ, our Saviour, was wrapped. They were putting up decorations in preparation for the festival to celebrate the Shroud. We left and made our way to the royal palace, passing yet more guards standing at the door. There is a great courtyard inside, decorated with statues and very fine architecturally. Further on one comes to a lovely garden with bronze and marble fountains. They are adorned with beautiful figures and have ample water.

*everything in the world, a broad
mirror in which we shall see the
most illustrious deeds of the great
royal house, with lifelike effigies
of each one of them. As we move
along we shall be instructed in all
the main fields of learning. On the
ceiling you will see forty-eight images of the heavens, the movement
of the heavens, planets and stars;
the mathematical and cosmograph-
ical forms of the earth and the seas,
and representations of all animals,
terrestrial, marine and aerial. It
will be greater than the greatest
intellect that may contemplate
it.' (L'idea de' Pittori, Scultori
et Architetti, 1607.) Zuccaro's
arcade had been demolished by
the early nineteenth century.*

There are enormous urns, all of them bronze, and so many it is impossible to count them. They contain orange and lemon trees and jasmine, and other sweet-scented plants and flowers. We were amazed to see so much variety.[a]

We went back to the courtyard. It has two broad flights of steps, which we ascended in order to see the royal apart-ments. They are superbly appointed and testify to the em-inence of this noble court. We saw the new chapel which is being built for the Holy Shroud. It is octagonal with black marble columns and a dome of the same material. The col-umns which support the dome have pedestals, bases, and capitals and there is a cornice all round. There are splendid figures all in bronze.[b]

When we left the palace we went straight to the new square, the Piazza San Carlo.[c] This is truly one of the finest squares I have ever seen. In shape it is a perfect square and is surrounded by very large and beautiful mansions of the kind that are now being built in this quarter of the city

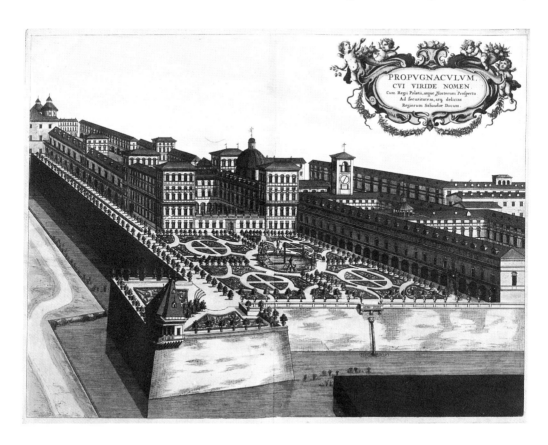

TURIN TO THE DAUPHINÉ

A *The farthest corner of the gardens overlooked the city wall and its moat. They even extended over a great bastion, high and steep-sided, which became known popularly as the 'green bastion'.*

B *The chapel was built between 1668 and 1694 and was designed by the architect Guarino Guarini. The shroud is kept in an etched silver casket and stands on an altar behind gold-plated grilles.*

C *Begun in 1640.*

D *The Roman Emperor Augustus named the city Augusta Taurinorum, the imperial city of the bulls. According to Pliny (Hist. Nat. XXXVII, iii, 21) the inhabitants were known as Taurini, being descended from a Ligurian tribe whose emblem was a bull. It has remained a device on the city's coat of arms to this day. The market was held in the former Piazza delle Erbe, which has now been built over. The 'Civic Tower' was demolished during Napoleon's occupation. The town hall, which overlooked the square, stood on the site of the present Palazzo di Città in the Via Milano, which was completed in the mid-eighteenth century.*

Fig. 12 *The Royal Palace, Turin, its gardens and, in the foreground, the 'green bastion'. (Engraved from a drawing by Tommaso Borgonio, 1665-6. Archivio Storico, Turin.)*

with splendid avenues. And what is so admirable, all the buildings are of the same style of architecture. There is a strongly-manned citadel here. At some public festivals the whole body of musketeers will fire a salute.

Then we returned through the town, which is really very fine and has a famous university. We came to the market place, which has a veritable abundance of everything. The town hall of the Commune of Turin stands here. At the far end of the square is a tower which was restored in 1667. It is all decorated with very fine figurative scenes. On the top of the tower is a splendid, large royal crown, cleverly contrived. It serves as a kind of pinnacle, or dome, for the tower and has a great bull on top. This represents the crown of His Royal Highness. The bull is taken from the city's coat of arms.[d]

Next we went to look for the palace of Monsignor Angelo Ranuzzi, a Bolognese nobleman. He is the archbishop of Diamata and Apostolic Nuncio at the court of HRH Carlo Emanuele, the Duke of Savoy and Prince of Piedmont. He performed many courtesies and kindnesses for us, and wanted us to lodge with him. When he departed he prepared passports and letters of recommendation for us, addressed to Mgr Borromei, Apostolic Nuncio to His Catholic Majesty, the King of Spain.

But before leaving the city we wanted to see the great festival which takes place in the royal piazza, when the Holy Shroud is displayed. When we arrived in the square we found it already filled with thousands of people. There were raised platforms round the square, similarly crowded. We managed to reach one end and, with great exertion, climbed up on it, where we rested and looked around with astonishment. The square was full of people, and so were the platforms, balconies, windows and roofs of the houses and mansions. Soldiers, on foot and on horseback, were all lined up in the middle of the square. The citadel was also full, its walls and gatehouses manned. Turin, though it is a fine city, is quite small and now, being so full, half the people had to remain outside. The well-drilled army stood on both sides of the central arcade. Then the procession began.

They carried the Shroud from the main chapel of the cathedral, through the royal palace and then down the arcade. In the middle they halted under a great baldachin

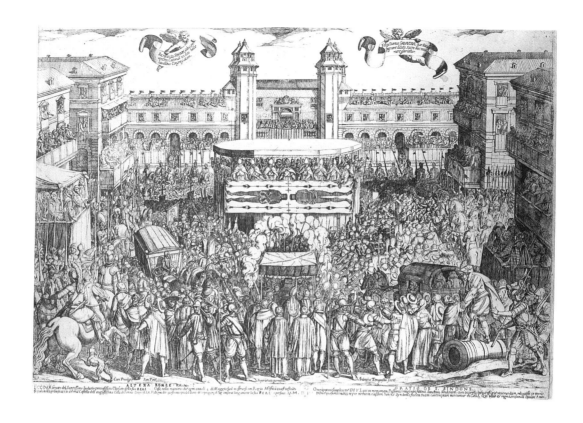

In the possession of the dukes of Savoy since 1453, the Holy Shroud was brought to Turin in 1578 from Chambéry, the former capital of the duchy. A special feast of the Holy Shroud, instituted by Pope Julius II early in the 16th century, was celebrated annually in Turin on 4 May when it was exposed to the people in front of the Palazzo Madama, in the ceremony that Laffi witnessed. Subsequently it was shown much less often and by the 20th century its public exposure had virtually ceased. In 1670, the year of Laffi's visit, the Pope granted plenary indulgence to all who made the pilgrimage to Turin in order to venerate it. Latest research has cast serious doubt on the Shroud's authenticity.

that covered a railed-off area. Here, in the sight of all the people, they unwound the holy relic, which had an infinite number of turns. This was done by seven bishops wearing full canonicals. Behind them was His Royal Highness, then the Apostolic Nuncio and all the other ambassadors. After an excellent and devout sermon had been delivered by a priest, everyone knelt, gazing at the Holy Shroud, which was stained with the very blood of our Saviour. Everyone wept, begging aloud to be forgiven their sins, and then crossed themselves.

Then we heard the musketeers firing a salute. The shots whistled through the air, sounding as if they too were weeping at the sight of the holy and bloody relic. From the surrounding walls and from the troops on both sides, the holy relic was saluted with threefold salvoes, until the air became so thick with smoke that you could no longer distinguish one person from another. Then the clocks began to strike the hour, after the French fashion, as in France and Spain.[a]

TURIN TO THE DAUPHINÉ

Fig. 13   *The exposure of the Holy Shroud in 1613 in the presence of Carlo Emanuele I and St Francis of Sales. (Engraved by Antonio Tempesta. Galleria Sabauda, Turin.)*

Fig. 14   *The royal palace of the Dukes of Savoy, Rivoli, destroyed in 1706. (Engraved from a drawing by Tommaso Borgonio, 1665-6. Archivio Storico, Turin.)*

After that, as we wanted to leave Turin, we went to take leave of the Apostolic Nuncio who, as I told you, had granted us passports and letters of recommendation, and who now also procured health certificates for us. Once outside the city gates we took the road to Rivoli, but before we got there a furious storm broke out. It poured down and there was such a fearful gale we barely escaped being swept up into the air. We arrived at a village called San Michele and went into an inn where we dried ourselves. Then we continued to Rivoli, which is five miles from Turin. It is a fortified town situated on a little hill, on the highest point of which is the great royal palace. We went on to Sant'Ambrogio, nine miles away. This place lies at the foot of very high hills; and seeing the sun sinking into the hills, we kept going in order to arrive there in good time. Here we lodged in a hovel – it was so mean, you could not call it an inn. All we had to eat were a few chestnuts, with water to drink, and we had to sleep on a great heap of dried leaves. Next morning we continued on to San Giorio, seven miles from

NOTARUM EXPLICATIO.

1. Arx Cavata.
2. Castrum Regum Gottrorum.
3. Templum Canonicor. Regul. Metrop.
4. Arcus Augusti.
5. Templum et Abbatia S. Iusti.
6. Templum S. Ioannis Baptistæ.
7. Cænobium S. Francisci.
8. Cænobium Capucinorum.
9. Templum S. Caroli. Sodal. Nom. Iesu.

10. Ecclesia Parochialis S. Pauli.
11. Ecclesia Paroch S. Russi.
12. Sacellum S. Auæ.
13. Templum Parochiale S. Martini.
14. Nosocomium B.V.
15. Templum B.V. Gratiarum.
16. Sacellum S. Sebastiani.
17. Templum B.V. Coronatæ Sodalitatum Spiritus Sancti.
18. Curia Episcopalis antiqua.
19. Curia, et Palatium Parlamenti.

20. Sacellum B.V. Gratiarum.
21. Forum.
22. Porta Sabaudica.
23. Porta Gallica.
24. Porta Taurinensis.
25. Porta antiqua ad Suppetias urbis.
26. Duria Fl.
27. Census Fl.
28. Palatium Cardin-Ostiensis.
29. Turris Publica.

Infidelstani Exc. Ioa...

38   TURIN TO THE DAUPHINÉ

Susa was the last town of any size for travellers going west over the Alps. On the next stage of the journey Laffi and his companion would find the going more difficult and dangerous, and a test of their courage and endurance. They arrived at the French frontier sooner than the traveller today. In Laffi's time it lay not far beyond Susa, in the foothills of the mountains. The present frontier, at the pass of Montgenèvre, was fixed in 1713 by the Treaty of Utrecht, when French territory was ceded to Savoy.

Sant'Ambrogio, keeping beside a wide river, until we reached Bussoleno, only six miles from San Giorio. From here we continued in the direction of Susa, a distance of four miles.[a]

Susa is a fairly large town, completely encircled by a wall that has big, very tall towers and a castle. It is a beautiful, very delightful place and has an abundance of everything. The mountain known as Mont Cenis begins to rise here. It is one of the very highest mountains. Two miles further on is a little town called Mollare. From there we kept going up for a few miles until we reached a large, splendid inn with many houses around it. This is the last town in Italy and in the state, or province, of Piedmont, belonging to the Duke of Savoy. Beyond this town, on the left hand, no further than a musket shot and no more then four paces from the roadside, stands a great signpost. On the eastern side it has the arms of Italy, on the west, those of France. But it is so old and so weather-worn that it is impossible to see what is carved on the arms, still less can you read the ancient inscription below. This post marks the boundary dividing France and Italy. At this point you enter the Dauphiné, and from here onwards we shall refer to distances in terms of leagues, one league being three Italian miles.

Fig. 15 *Detail of a view of Susa. (Engraved from a drawing by Tommaso Borgonio, 1665-6. Archivio Storico, Turin.)*

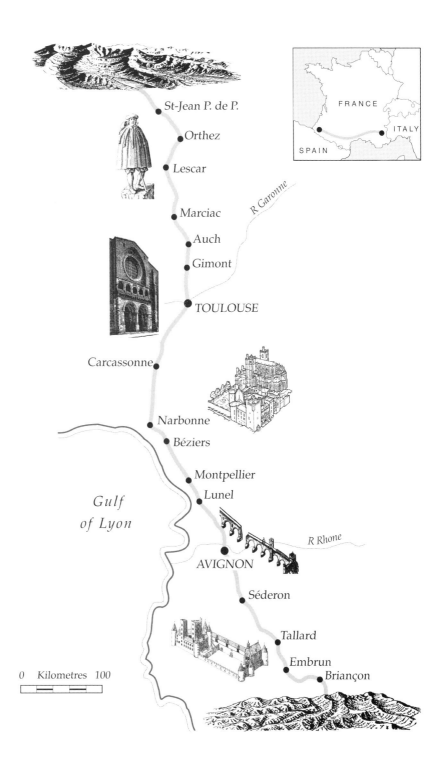

St-Jean P. de P.

Orthez

Lescar

Marciac

Auch

Gimont

TOULOUSE

Carcassonne

Narbonne

Béziers

Montpellier

Lunel

Gulf of Lyon

AVIGNON

Séderon

Tallard

Embrun

Briançon

R Garonne

R Rhone

FRANCE

ITALY

SPAIN

0   Kilometres   100

Fig. 16 *The chateau of Tallard,*
early 17th century.

CHAUMONT TO AVIGNON

4

THROUGH THE DAUPHINÉ
Chaumont to Avignon

A *Laffi's route over the Alps was one of the historic highways between Italy and France. The pass of Montgenèvre is one of the lowest in the Alps, about 6000 ft. It was used by the armies of ancient Rome, of Charlemagne and in French campaigns in northern Italy. Italian pilgrims going to Compostella preferred to go to that way instead of taking the road round the Gulf of Genoa. The coast road, although shorter, was, until the eighteenth century, continually threatened by Mediterranean pirates.*

The fortress of Exilles is typical of Piedmontese strongholds designed to obstruct invaders. Much of it still stands, and the terrain thereabouts is broadly as Laffi describes it.

B *Dora di Bardonecchia and Dora Riparia.*

AFTER CROSSING THE ITALIAN FRONTIER you come to a pleasant place called Chaumont, the first village in France. It lies between rugged peaks. Another two leagues and you reach a broad river, the Dora, where you cross a wooden bridge and climb to a fortified town called Exilles. This town is situated on a rocky promontory between two precipitous peaks, and thus forms a natural island. On one side is the river, fast flowing because of the water from the perpetual snows in these mountains. On the other is a very steep mountain-side. At this point the passage between the town and the rock face is narrow enough for them to have built two strong gatehouses with high walls, through which you have to pass.[a]

We entered the first gate, which the guards closed behind us, so that we were, as it were, imprisoned between the two gates. The guards questioned us as to where we came from, and where we were going. They asked to see our passports and health certificates, which we produced. Then, straight away, one of the soldiers led us into the town, up a stairway that had been cut in the rock. He took us before the castellan who asked the same questions and, likewise, wanted to see our passports and health certificates. Having seen them he allowed us to continue on our way.

On leaving the town we were accompanied by this same soldier until we were outside the second gate. We tipped the guards and resumed our journey towards Oulx. This town is in a plain into which two wide rivers flow,[b] and lies between two high mountain ranges. It has everything in plenty. There is a hospice attached to a very large monastery, occupied by the canons of an order founded by St Francis de Sales. They wear a black habit with a white

A *The people of Oulx today still
pronounce it 'Ours' (bear), though
Laffi's etymology should not be
taken too seriously.*

silk band hanging down from the shoulders in the same
way as a scapular. They looked after pilgrims very well, and
gave us food and shelter. The town is very agreeable because of its fountains and fine buildings. Going along the
main street we observed, nailed up and hanging above the
doors of the grandest houses, huge bear-skins – in truth! –
that had been killed in the chase. There were also a few
wild boars, which are very plentiful in this region. It is for
this reason that the town is called 'Ours'.*a* We lodged here
for the night.

We departed early the next morning and began to climb
once more. We kept beside the river for a distance of two
leagues until we reached Cesana. This town is bigger and
finer than Oulx. As we entered we saw a long procession of
men and women, led by a priest. Behind him was a well-
dressed young man, alone, carrying a great bunch of
flowers and foliage. After him came other men walking two
by two, also bearing masses of greenery. Behind the men
there followed a young woman, similarly well turned out,
also carrying flowers and leaves. After her came other women, likewise in twos. Out of curiosity we followed the procession to see where it would end. They entered the main
church, dividing into two files, the men on one side and the
women on the other. The priest went up to the altar, while
the young man sat on a stool. The young woman sat on
another beside him, a little apart. We supposed that this
was to be some sort of wedding, as indeed it proved to be.
When the ecclesiastical ceremonies were over, we approached the priest and asked if we might say Mass, to
which he kindly consented. After it was finished, with all
those people being present to hear it, they invited us to join
them at their table. So we too now took part in the procession, which went off in the same order as before. Except
that, instead of holding bunches of flowers and leaves, we
had our long pilgrim's staves in our hands, rather like two
pikestaffs. In this manner we wound our way through the
town, to our great merriment. Indeed it was quite an effort
to contain our laughter, to see such a singular thing.

At length, after much going round and about, we arrived
with this large company at the bridegroom's house. Inside,
long tables had been set out and, after many formalities,
alla francese, everyone sat down in the order of their arrival.
Eventually it came to our turn and we took our place at the

last of the tables, because we were the last to be invited. So we settled down cheerfully, but could now no longer contain our mirth because we could not understand a word they were saying.[b]

When the banquet was over everyone stood up. A big empty bowl was brought in and given to the bride. First of all she went round to her father, mother, and family to collect money by way of gifts. It is called the 'bride's gift', and serves as her dowry. Next, she went round to all her friends who were her guests. They all gave her, little or much, according to their ability. When we saw that she was approaching everyone we no longer wanted to laugh. We told ourselves we found no pleasure in being their guests if it was a question of having to pay. However we cheered up when the bride reached us. As we were searching for a little money to give her, she chid us, saying she did not want it. Instead, taking a handful of coins from the bowl she gave them to us, asking us to offer prayers to God on her behalf. The bridegroom did the same. Hence we prayed to our Lord that he might often grant us these opportunities, because such customs greatly please us.

We thanked them and left Cesana in good spirits to begin the great climb to Montgenèvre. It is extremely dangerous. One goes between great crags and sheer rock faces which, by the look of them, are about to fall. The ravine is about two leagues long and indeed strikes terror in everyone, because of the many who have been killed by avalanches and broken fragments that are continually falling from the mountain. They lie entombed beneath the snow and ice and the great rocks that cover the whole footpath. It is only by God's grace that one passes through this place. After many difficulties and feeling intolerably weary we reached the top, where there is a town called Monginevro. It is quite big, and was still covered with ice and snow. Here they dispense the *passada* to pilgrims, consisting of bread and wine. The commune doles out this charity to all pilgrims who pass through this harsh region, if they have no money.

Another two leagues and we came into Briançon where we stayed the night. Next morning, after saying Mass in the principal church, we left for Embrun, passing the village of St-Martin, two leagues, then St-Michel, and then St-Crépin, another three leagues. All these villages are built of

A *The ruins of the medieval battle-ments can still be seen above the escarpment, and there is evidence of the double wall. The river is the Durance. Its present course is some distance from the foot of the escarpment.*

B *Probably the Avance, a tributary of the Durance.*

C *Not identified.*

wood and roofed in the same material. They lie at the bottom of a river valley between mountain ranges, and therefore enjoy little sun. It appears during the morning over the peaks of very high mountains that are always snow-covered. As we made our way towards Embrun night began to fall while we still had about four leagues to go, so we stopped at a village called Chateauroux. Early next morning we reached the town of Embrun. We went immediately to the bishop to have him sign our patents so that we could say Mass, which we then celebrated in the cathedral. The town is surrounded by a double wall and is very big. It stands on a hill above a great escarpment. Below, is a broad, fast running river, making it impregnable on that side.[a]

From here we took the road to Chorges, four leagues from Embrun. After Chorges you come to another village called Selara, and after that, St-Étienne-le-Laus. Here we found lodgings, worn out after a tiring journey when we had been buffeted by the wind. In the morning we set off for the next village where we would say Mass. On arrival, we found it was a feast day, so we asked for the parish priest but they replied that there was none. So we went on towards Cenasa. Before we got there we came to a great, fast-flowing river.[b] We tested the depth with our staves meaning to wade across, but found it was greater than a man's height. The speed and depth of the water seemed to make any passage impossible for us. But, as we were standing anxiously on the bank, we noticed many pine trees that had been felled and trimmed, waiting to be floated away down the river. As some bold action was called for, with great effort we rolled one into the water. Thus it served us as a bridge by which to cross. But it was not without the obvious risk of our being drowned, for when we reached the middle, the tree trunk sank and we were up to our waists in water. Had not the glorious St James saved us by a miracle, we should certainly have been lost. So, we emerged from danger, having looked death in the face with pounding hearts, and dried ourselves best as we could in the sun.

Then we entered the town of Cenasa.[c] It was a pitiful sight. The houses were either half destroyed by fire or partly blown down by the wind. Some were in ruins because of the huge rocks that had been dislodged from the mountainside and fallen sheer upon the town, which lay in the valley bottom. We made our way round the ruins seek-

'console' – in the Middle Ages, the magistrate of the commune was known as a consul, whose functions were juridical and administrative.

ing, among the few buildings that remained standing, a church where we might say Mass. At the end of one street we heard singing, so we supposed that there must be some church or chapel nearby. Going in the direction of the singing, we saw a little church – or rather, it was more like a winter refuge from the snow than a chapel, because it was roofed with thatch and built simply of bricks, without whitewash or any kind of decoration.

We entered and found a few country-folk singing the Office of the Blessed Virgin, but they sang so badly we did not know whether to be angry or to laugh. They were standing around by their benches like so many donkeys. When the service was over we asked if we might say Mass. They agreed and immediately handed us the instruments. The altar stood in such a narrow niche that I had great trouble in reaching it and was so small that the missal almost entirely covered it. Thus, the server had to hold it half off the altar. The altar itself was made of boards roughly joined together, which kept shaking about. I have never in all my days been so disconcerted. Even so, with the help of God, I celebrated.

When Mass was over I approached one of these rustics who indicated to us in his own tongue that we might take a meal with him. After exchanging a few courtesies we agreed. He led us to his house and had a table set, where we ate with good cheer. But when we had finished the meal, which we thought was for nothing, he made it quite plain that he wanted to be paid for it. His place was an inn, he explained. So we had no alternative and, contrary to what we were expecting, we paid him. Then we left for Tallard, four leagues from Cenasa.

Tallard is a pleasant, populous and well-fortified town. It lies in a fertile plain of great charm, and has an abundance of everything. It is surrounded by strong walls. In the middle of the square is a large well, which serves all the inhabitants. The mouth of the well is all of one piece, carved out of stone. It is very big and is a wonderful sight. Opposite is the local magistrate's[d] place. Here he gives a *passada* to all pilgrims, that is to say, alms of so much money.

Then there is the house of the local lord, a most remarkable building. It is very large and is built on rising ground so that it overlooks all the other houses. The architecture is very striking. It is very high and has as many windows

A *The chateau of Tallard was begun in the fourteenth century and completed at the beginning of the sixteenth. It is certainly a curiosity. Laffi's reference to the number of windows, doors and towers was based on an old local tradition. It was also said that there were as many steps as there are hours in the year. None of this can now be verified because the building was severely damaged by fire in 1692, though a contemporary engraving suggests that there were fewer than twelve towers. It is today being restored. The chateau has a double chapel, one built immediately above the other, the lower one being excavated in the rock. The axis of the chapels is, unusually, north-west/south-east, the altar in the upper chapel having been placed at the north-west end, and the one in the lower chapel at the south-east end. It is known that special offices were celebrated at the winter and summer solstices. The celebrant would face the rising sun in winter in the lower chapel, and the setting sun in summer in the upper. It seems that we have here vestiges of an ancient pagan cult of the sun over which Christian rituals were later superimposed. It is also conjectured that the building as a whole may have been designed to reflect the seasonal nature of this worship, which could explain the curious tradition concerning the number of windows, doors, etc. See Aimès, P., 'Le château de Tallard',* Bulletin de la Société d'Études des Hautes-Alpes, *1955.*

B *The Céans.*

as there are days in the year, as many rooms as there are weeks, and as many towers (which are like bell-towers) as there are months. Even from a distance it is a splendid sight, but seen closed at hand it is a truly superb edifice. Among the many castles that I have seen throughout the whole of France, this is the finest.[a]

After leaving the town gate we found a spring of cool water where we refreshed ourselves. Then we took the road to La Saulce, one league from Tallard. This is a big town, lying on the slopes of a hill, and is crowded with vines and orchards with all kinds of fruit. Here, too, they give the *passada*, as in almost all French towns. From here we went to Lazer, another three leagues, where we found good, cheap lodgings. This town is the last in the Dauphiné. Next morning we arrived at Orpierre, two leagues from Lazer. This is the first town of Provence, and lies in a cleft between two very steep-sided mountains. A huge river runs at the bottom,[b] which can be crossed at no other place except this town. There are many vineyards and orchards with all kinds of fruit. They lie across the river, which is used to irrigate them. There are also many charming pleasure gardens, where people can enjoy all kinds of diversions and pastimes. From Orpierre to Séderon is three leagues. On leaving the town we climbed very high and very steeply, until midday. On reaching the top of this steep hill-side we were tired out and bathed in sweat. But there was a high cliff, which we now made for in order to rest in its shade. At the foot of the cliff there gushed a spring of cool water where we refreshed ourselves, thanking God for this good fortune.[c]

Then we descended on the other side in the direction of Séderon. On reaching the bottom of the hill we came to a wide river.[d] We had to take our shoes off in order to cross, and then only managed it with much difficulty. The water was deep and it was also still cold because it came down from the snows on these high mountains. We reached the other side and went on to Séderon. Séderon is situated beside a river that runs through these barren mountains. There is not a single tree nor even a blade of grass to be seen because the mountain slopes are of bare rock. When you enter the town you cross a big bridge, consisting of a single span that reaches from one bank to the other. We spent the night here in an inn. The town is half in ruins

C *The spring still runs. It is called 'La source Guilliny', and is just over the Pass of St-Jean, between Orpierre and Séderon. There is another, a little lower down the hill.*

D *The Méouge.*

E *Sault today still has some remains of the old fortifications. One or two of the round bastions have survived, converted into dwellings. The flight of steps can be traced right down to the river. It is mostly no more than a steep pathway today, though a few roughly-hewn steps, cut in the rock, still remain.*

because of landslides in the mountains. It often happens that huge boulders fall, knocking down houses. We lodged here, though very unwillingly, but got no sleep, anxious lest a rock might fall on us.

From here we continued on to Sault, a distance of three leagues. But we had hardly left Séderon before we had to climb a high and very steep hill. On reaching the top we found a well, hewn from a rock, where there were many women drawing water. They gave us some to drink. Then we descended on the other side into a broad plain of fields and woodlands. We found another well here, but now we were alone. So, in order to drink – our thirst drove us to it – we tied our staves together, end to end, with a hat on one end. By this means we were able to draw up water. Having drunk, we went on many miles through a great forest until we finally reached Sault. This place is situated on top of a rocky promontory. Below is a fast-flowing river which, after heavy rain, floods the plain, causing much damage. It is a splendid town, well fortified and not very large. It is surrounded by a high wall with many round towers. They are a fine sight. We saw the principal church which is old and has some beautiful, well-painted pictures. It also has a relic of St Anne. After seeing round the town, we left by a gate where you descend a flight of many steps cut in the rock, until you reach flat ground at river level.*

From here we climbed again over a distance of three leagues. On reaching a pass we found an inn where we refreshed ourselves. Then we began to descend once more for about the same distance, through rocks and landslides. Many colours are revealed, visible in certain veins in the layers of rock. They are like a rainbow, of the same varied and beautiful colours. Soon we came to Mormoiron, the first town in the county of Avignon. It is very large, ringed with walls and lies in a beautiful, flat countryside where there are trees bearing every kind of fruit. We liked this place very much. There are big olive groves, some in the plain and some on the mountain slopes.

Here, as everywhere in the county of Avignon, one hears the townsfolk telling of a very curious happening, which is this: whenever the Holy See stands vacant, the *sede vacante* as it is called, following the death of a Pope, all the olive trees dry up and drop their leaves until a new pontiff has been elected. Whether this be true I do not know, though, for sure, when we ourselves were passing through the county, we saw with our own eyes that they were all stripped of leaves, and this was during the *sede vacante* following the death of Clement IX. Whether, on the election of Clement X, they once more turned green I cannot offer any evidence, for by then I was no longer in this region.

We took lodgings outside the town gates in order to be able to continue our journey early next morning. After depositing our baggage at an inn and telling the host he should prepare supper, we went for a walk through the town. We saw houses, mansions, some not very outstanding churches and a small square. We returned to the inn and early next morning set off for Carpentras, three leagues away, travelling all the while through a fine, broad plain. On entering Carpentras we went to the main square, where the royal guard is stationed. There are many garrison companies in this city, who provide guards for the city gates and walls. They have all kinds of fruit in plenty here, and bread and wine in particular. In the middle of the square is a splendid fountain which gushes water abundantly. And there are quantities of lemons. We left Carpentras and made for Monteux, which lies further on. This place has a fine city wall with soldiers guarding the gates. Having seen it we continued on our way, keeping all the time on the level, as far as Entraigues, two leagues from Carpentras.

This is a strongly fortified town, built on a promontory, though not very high, and likewise surrounded by a good wall. There are some fine buildings, including the castle of the local lord, which has beautiful gardens. This nobleman gives a *passada* of much money to pilgrims who are going to Galicia.[a] From here we followed fine, broad roads across level countryside until we reached the beautiful city of Avignon. But there was a roaring wind that blows continually over the region. The local people say that should there be a year when the wind does not blow, then next year they can harvest nothing, neither corn nor fruit. Therefore they quote a Latin proverb: *Avenio ventosa, sine vento venenosa,* which means 'Windy Avignon, without the wind it is unhealthy'.[b] However that may be, there are many people who maintain it is true.

5

LAURA, HERETICS

& A PILGRIM SAINT

Avignon to Narbonne

A *The guards at the gate and the officers whom Laffi would meet later were all Italians, because Avignon at that time was part of the papal state, the County of Venaissin, and the city was garrisoned with Italian troops. It was governed by the Pope's representative, the vice-legate. Though the last Pope (or 'antipope') had left Avignon in 1403 the territory was not restored to France until the Revolution. The citizens of Avignon rebelled more than once against their often oppressive Italian masters, as Laffi tells later.*

WHEN WE REACHED THE GATE OF AVIGNON the toll-gatherer asked us where we came from and where we were going. We said we had come from Italy and were going to Galicia, so he let us through the first portcullis. When we reached the second, a sentry asked us the same questions. He then let us go forward to a gatehouse where there is a guard room. Here, a corporal repeated the above questions and, noticing that we were Italians, asked us many things about Italy. Meanwhile a Bolognese soldier arrived whom I recognized. He was a man with whom I had travelled in Spain on other occasions. He embraced us warmly, telling us he had only recently come to Avignon. He also said a new Pope had now been elected, Cardinal Altieri, who was called Clement X, and we were very pleased about this. As it was now evening he took us to an inn.[a]

Next morning, having washed and dressed for the city in good time, we went to the palace. It stands on top of a great rock in the middle of the city. The cathedral was built on the same rock base, so as to adjoin the palace. At the palace gate is a very large, double guard, the first with foot soldiers at the portcullis, the second with mounted cavalry at the gate. The latter are all noblemen and are called the Light Guard of the vice-legate.

The palace is built in the ancient style and is constructed entirely of masonry. It is very high and has great towers, and is altogether a magnificent sight. Next we went into the cathedral, which is also very old and likewise built of stone. In front of it is a large square, paved with the same material. The interior of the church is filled with antiquities. There are big, splendid tombs of many Popes, made of the finest marble. They were buried here when the see of St Peter was transferred to this city, where it remained for a long time. We went through into a cloister where there are many tombs of marble and other materials, the resting places of Popes, cardinals, archbishops, bishops and other eminent men.

We climbed the grand staircase to the office of the vicar-general to have a dimissory letter signed so that we could celebrate Mass. After the signing we went to look for Signor Cavaliere F. Giulio Bovio, a Bolognese nobleman who held the office of captain of the militia to His Holiness. We

Fig. 17 *The bridge of Avignon in 1618. (Bibliothèque Municipale, Avignon, estampe atlas 96, vues 1 and 2.)*

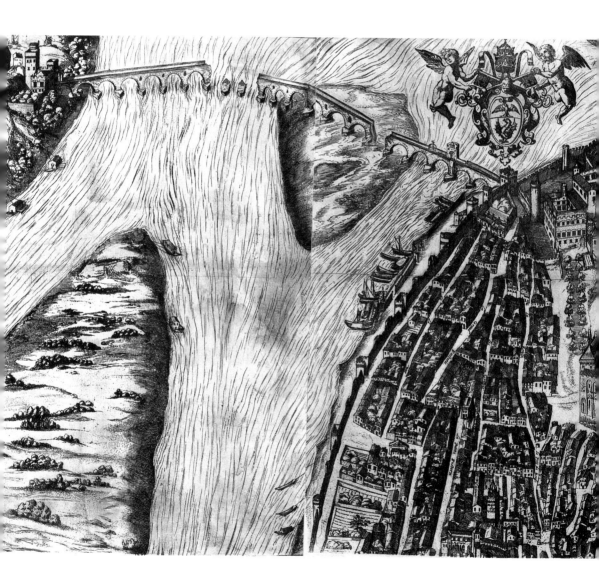

A *Jean Bénézet, after whom the bridge is named, founded a confraternity about 1177 to organize the building work. It included a hospital beside the bridge, which cared for pilgrims and other travellers. Bénézet died in 1184, just before the work was completed and was buried in the chapel on the bridge. By 1202 he was already being referred to as Saint Bénézet or, as Laffi calls him, Benedict. From that time legends began to accumulate about him. Though the bridge was partly rebuilt later, it crumbled seriously in 1670 and Bénézet's body was moved for safety to the hospital chapel, which had recently been enlarged and decorated in his honour. It would have been here that Laffi saw the miracle depicted. Of some fifteen or sixteen paintings only one has survived. It is now in the hospital of St Martha. In 1674 the body was again moved, this time to the Celestine convent. The tomb disappeared during the Revolution when the convent was laid waste and abandoned.*

presented him with a letter given to us in Bologna by his brother. This gentleman welcomed us warmly, asking us about things in Bologna, and what news we brought from our homeland. We told him what was happening at the present time in Bologna. Then he gave us a man to conduct us round the whole city of Avignon, to show us its most outstanding features. After that we went to St-Agricol to celebrate Mass, and afterwards to dine with the Bolognese nobleman. He had also invited other guests and he treated us very lavishly. When the meal was over we went with his priest round the city once more and saw many very fine churches. They are all built in the ancient style and contain many antiquities. This town has a university which is very well attended.

Next, we went out of the city gate that is towards the Rhône and saw the large and beautiful marble bridge. Four arches have fallen because of the strong current. There is a little chapel on the bridge, which once housed the body of a certain St Benedict, a shepherd boy who wrought this miracle. There was a child who told a lie, but who swore that if what he said was not truth, then his head would be turned back to front – which was what suddenly happened! The wretched child had recourse to prayer in the saint's chapel, and was restored. The saint, as I just said, used to be on the bridge, but they took him into the city lest the rest of the bridge fall and the holy body be swept away. When the body was brought into the city people crowded in to see it. At the place where I saw it, the whole of the above miracle is depicted.[a]

We took a turn round the city walls. They really are splendid, having been built of great square stones, all the same size. All round the battlements there are many very large towers. On the inside is a parapet walk for the sentries. It is supported on projecting masonry, or rather, one should say, on corbels. It makes a wonderful sight. The walls alone, if I may say so, are worth seeing as much as all the rest of the city. They are surrounded by a wide and very deep moat. On the inside you can see very tall and very old bell-towers, and they have very good bells.

When evening came, we walked a little way through the different quarters of the town, guided by one of our soldier friends of the Light Guard who, as I said, are all cavalrymen. He was Captain Lorenzo Orselli, who came from Forlì. He made us welcome and plied us with the best wines

Laffi now reveals a taste for the macabre, a sentiment shared by many in those days. The painting belonged to a genre that had been popularized as a result of the plague. The series of calamities that swept Europe in the 14th century led to a preoccupation with death that eventually expressed itself in art in a variety of allegorical themes. They were meant to persuade the spectator to reflect upon human mortality and the vanity of earthly things. A decaying corpse was a not uncommon feature of such works.

———

Fig. 18 *The tomb of Cardinal Legrange, early 15th century, (Musée du Petit Palais.)*

and other delicacies. We went out with him in the company of some young ladies of rank from that quarter, as is the French custom. After a while we took our leave of this gentleman and returned to our inn. In the morning we took a short walk through the city to see its churches and palaces. We went into the Jesuit church which has a pulpit of marvellous materials, workmanship and beauty. We also went to see the Carthusian church, which is truly charming, and from there to the church of the Celestines, called St-Pierre-de-Luxembourg. We looked round the church and its very fine and well-endowed monastery. It possesses one really remarkable thing that is well worth seeing, particularly by the faithful. This is a large picture painted by King René, Count of Provence. It is an excellent picture, as good as the work of our Bolognese painters, the Carracci. The king kept no other paintings but this, burning all others so that this one might be unique in all the world, as indeed it is.[a]

The painting depicts a dead man, standing up, having just emerged from a wooden coffin. The coffin, which is drawn in exact perspective, leans against a large cross. This

B *By the vermin.*

C *René, Count of Provence and king of Sicily and Naples (1409-80), was a patron of poets, musicians and painters, and was himself a man of varied talents. An old tradition attributed this painting to him, which was supposed to represent his mistress. It was said that, overcome by her death, he determined to have one last glimpse of her and reopened her tomb. The shock of what he saw inspired the painting. Laffi's reference to a male body is curious. It can scarcely be a deliberate bowdlerisation since he commends the picture particularly to the devout. Until the Revolution it hung in the Celestines' convent, which then had one of the richest collections of works of art in Avignon. It was known as 'La toile d'araignée', the 'Spiders' Web', or 'Portrait de la Mort', and was one of most celebrated works in the collection. It was lost when the convent was sacked.*

D *This was the mausoleum of Cardinal Legrange, who died some time after 1402. It was erected in the choir of the church of St-Martial ('St-Mercuriale' appears to be a slip of the pen). It was destroyed during the Revolution but its details have fortunately been preserved in a seventeenth-century drawing. It was certainly a monument every bit as remarkable as Laffi describes. It consisted of five sections, one above the other, of biblical scenes, as well as three representations of the cardinal himself in various guises. Several fragments of the sculpture can be seen in the Petit*

indicates that the place may well be a cemetery, with the cross in the middle. As I say, the coffin is in perspective and placed so that you can see everything inside. In it you can see what has come out of the corpse – snakes, scorpions, worms, spiders' webs and dust. It is all done in such a realistic way that they seem to be alive and moving about in the coffin. Parts of the dead man's body are missing because they have been eaten.[b] He, as I said, is standing up, looking into the coffin, and indicating that he had got out of it because he could no longer bear the torment of these creatures. His flesh is all peeling and gnawed away, completely disfigured by them. Over his shoulder he has a piece of shroud, all torn, with bits falling from the back, so that it covers the body in only a few places. But it is depicted so naturally, you can hardly tell whether it is real or simulated. It is a most remarkable work, as much for the excellence of the painting as for the artist who did it. He, as I said, produced no other work except this one, and he is a king.[c]

From here we went to see the Benedictine monastery of St-Mercuriale. There are some fine things here, in particular, in the church a statue of a consumptive. It is something you might say goes almost beyond human skill. It is made of white marble and lies at the foot of a superb tomb. The tomb is so tall, it reaches the vault of the ceiling. The whole work is of white marble and is decorated with excellent figures in relief and in *mezzo-rilievo*. They are superb and should not be missed by anyone who is passing through this city.[d]

Next we went to see the monastery of the Franciscan Friars Minor – they belong to the Conventuals. We lodged with them for two nights, both on our way to Galicia and on our return. The third time I came to this city was in the company of Fra Giuseppe Liparini, of the same order. That was in the year 1673. It is a very fine Franciscan monastery. It is very old and its church surpasses all others in Avignon. The church is large, has a vaulted ceiling, and is built entirely of masonry. There is only the one nave so the vault is without columns. Yet it is unbelievably wide and of very considerable height. In this respect I have never seen another like it. The high altar is very pleasing and is well proportioned and well built. The chapels are well arranged and well looked after. In one of them, called the Holy Cross, is the tomb of the lady Laura, so greatly beloved by Petrarch.[a]

This lady was of the Masani family, nobles of Avignon, but was descended from a Florentine family. It is told how Petrarch, on learning of the death of his dear Laura, came post-haste from Paris to Avignon. On hearing that she had been buried in the Franciscan church, he went there next morning. He saw the tomb of his now dead beloved and, on returning home, seized a pen and composed a sonnet to his lady, so recently departed. He returned to the church at Vespers and remained there until nightfall, hidden under a bench and observed by no one. In the middle of the night he went to the tomb of the lady Laura and unsealed it. Then, taking a knife, he cut open her breast, which was still unwithered, and placed a lead box upon her heart. In it was a portrait of the lady, engraved likewise on lead, together with the sonnet, lately written by him on parchment. Then he closed the tomb again, hid himself as before and, when morning came, departed.[b]

Many years passed until, in 1533, Francis I, king of France, came to Avignon from Paris. After seeing round the city, which pleased him greatly, he asked to be shown its more noteworthy curiosities. Especially he wished to see the tomb of the lady Laura, who was so much lauded by Petrarch. He went to the church and saw the tomb, which he greatly admired. He read the epitaph, which goes as follows, for I too have seen it with my own eyes. I have copied it word for word so that you too, dear reader, may appreciate it:

ET MEMORIAE AETERNAE D. LAURA[c]
CUM PUDICITIA TUM FORMA FEM. INCOMPARABILIS.
QUAE TANDIU VIXIT, UT EIUS MEMORIAE NUNQUAM
EXTINGUI POSIT R.R. VETERAM MONUMENTORUM
PEREGRINORUM INDAGATUS D. CHRISTOPHORUS DE
ALEGRE EQUES LUSITANUS, D. ANTONIUS DE
PRAT PRAETOR PARISIENSIS, GABRIEL SIMONUS
FLORENTINUS, MAURITIUS SEVA.

After his majesty had read the epitaph, he had her tomb opened and gazed within. He looked upon that body which had once been both an image and a treasure-house of all the beauties in the world. But now, I have to tell you, he saw how it had become a horrid skeleton, stripped of all flesh

Palais Museum at Avignon, including the 'consumptive' in its entirety. It is not, as Laffi thought, a consumptive but represents the cardinal's emaciated body as it would have been soon after death. This was another example of the 'vanity of earthly things', which the accompanying inscription confirms: 'Let all, great or small, see to what estate they will be reduced. What cause for pride is there? For dust you are, and, like me, you will become a fetid corpse, the food of worms, and return to ashes.'

A Unfortunately, Laffi's romantic version of the events following Laura's death bears little or no relation to the facts, so far as they are known. By the time of his visit, the tomb had for long been a place of literary pilgrimage, the circumstances of its discovery were well known and even the question of her identity (still unresolved today) seemed to be settled. Yet for some reason Laffi accepted uncritically a different, palpably inaccurate story, which he presumably got from the Franciscans. Their church is now mostly a ruin, destroyed in the Revolution. The remains are incorporated in the Collège Saint-Joseph. The tomb is lost.

B Far from making an impulsive dash from Paris while his beloved's body was scarcely cold, Petrarch himself has recorded that he first had news of her death six weeks later while he was in Italy, at Parma. At the time of her death he was in Verona. The sonnet is generally regarded as a forgery. There is some evidence, mainly circumstantial, that Laura may be

identified with a daughter of
the de Noves family, who were
local nobility. She married Hugh
de Sade in 1325, died in 1348,
probably from the plague, and
was buried in the de Sade chapel
in the Franciscans' church.

c 'To Donna Laura of eternal
memory.' James Hogarth writes:
The inscription seems to be both
garbled and incomplete. To begin
with, there is no principal verb:
one would expect something like
'To DL of eternal memory this
memorial was set up by ...' It rather looks as if one or more lines
have been omitted at the beginning of the inscription (which
might explain the et, otherwise
uncalled for). Then the second
line ('a woman incomparable
both for chastity and for beauty')
is, oddly, in the nominative, where
one might expect a genitive. The
next nine words are straightfor-
ward ('who so lived that her memory can never be extinguished'),
though memoriae should be
memoria and posit should be
possit. In the next phrase R.R. is
puzzling, but might conceivably
be a contraction for reliquias,
'remains'. A noun in the accusat-
ive case is required to provide an
object for indagatus, 'having
studied' – which is in the singular,
though there are four 'signatories'!
– and a peg on which to hang the
genitive plurals veteram (so
spelt) monumentorum pere-
grinorum, 'of ancient foreign
monuments'. Altogether this is a
very peculiar piece of Latin.

The signatories are (Don)
Christoforo, Knight of Portugal,
(Don) Antoine de Prat, Gabriele
Simone, Florentine, and Maurice
Scève.

by the worms, all turned to dust and putrefaction, the
wretched remains left by vipers, toads and scorpions. Then,
peering among these dried up bones, he saw, between the
ribs in the place where the heart had once been once, a lead
box, locked and covered with the body's dust that lay all
about. Drawn by curiosity to investigate whatever secret
that little box might hold, he had it taken out and opened
there and then. In it he discovered the portrait and the
aforesaid sonnet.

I myself unfolded it and read it many times. I give below
the text, which I copied out from the original itself, because
I too was curious to see it. With me was the Franciscan, Fra
Giuseppe Liparini, whom I mentioned earlier and who was
my companion on that occasion. So, I saw it, held it in my
own hands and read it. I also admired the portrait very
much. It takes the form of a medallion, and has the following letters engraved round the edge: M.L.M.I., meaning
Madonna Laura Morta Iace, Here lies my lady Laura deceased.
The other side is blank. The box which contains it is now
kept in the sacristy of the Franciscan fathers, and is shown
to anyone who asks to see it. The sonnet is as follows:

> *Qui riposan quei caste & felici ossa*
> *Di quella alma gentile & sola in terra*
> *Aspro't dur sasso hor ben teco hai soterra*
> *El vero honor la fama e beltà Scossa*
> *Morte ha del verde Laura svelta e mossa*
> *Fresca radice e il premio de mia guerra*
> *Di quatro lustri: e piu se anchor non erra*
> *Mio penser tristo e il chiude in pocha fossa.*
> *Felice pianta: in borgo de Avignone*
> *Nacque e mori: & qui con ella jace*
> *La penna, el stil, l'inchiostro e la ragione.*
> *O delicate membra, o viva face*
> *Che anchor me cuoci e struggi inginocchione*
> *Ciascun prieghi il Signor te accepti in pace.*

[Here do repose those chaste and blessed bones
Of a spirit tender and unique on earth.
Hard stone! thou hast with thee beneath the earth
True honour, Fame and beauty! Death hath shaken,
Moved and uprooted from the laurel green

A *'Carmes' would appear to be a misprint, probably for 'Larmes'.*

Francis I's visit took place in September 1533 and the quatrains are probably his own. However, it was not he who made the discovery of the lead box and its contents. That had already happened some months earlier, and was probably that which prompted the king's visit. A humanist scholar, Maurice Scève, of Lyon, who was a student of Petrarch, had been conducting an extensive search for Laura's remains, with a group of companions. On opening the tomb in the Franciscan chapel, Scève was convinced that he had found what he sought. It is nowadays supposed that it was Scève who wrote the sonnet, in order to supply supporting evidence for his discovery (in which case the lead box, as he found it, would have held only the medallion). The meaning of the initials round the portrait, as given by Laffi, was first proposed by Scève, but is no longer taken seriously. The Latin epitaph, 'To Donna Laura of eternal memory,' appears to have been composed by Scève, whose name concludes the list of researchers. See further: Guidici, Enzo, 'Bilancio di una annosa questione: Maurice Scève e la "Scoperta" della "tomba di Laura"', Quaderni di Filologia e lingue romanze, vol. 2, Università di Macerata, 1980: also Daubigny, J., 'Pétrarque et le Vaucluse', Études Vauclusiennes, no. XXVI, July-Dec., 1981.

Its fresh root and the prize of my long strife
Of twenty years (and more, if my sad thought
Errs not) and shuts it in a narrow grave.
A blessed plant in town of Avignon
Was born and died, and here with her doth lie
The pen, the stylus, ink and power of thought.
O delicate limbs and thou, O living face,
Which dost inflame and slay me while I kneel,
Let each pray God He welcomes thee in peace.]

Then Francis I had the lady Laura's tomb put back in good order. He embellished it with various epitaphs, and he himself composed two quatrains, which he put in the box with Petrarch's verses. Since he was such an illustrious person it seems right that I should give them here:

CARMES DU ROY LE GRAND[a]
SUR LE TUMBEAU DE MADAM LAURE

En petit lieu compris vous pouvez voir
Ce qui comprent beaucoup par renommée
Plume, labeur, la langue & le savoir
Furent vaincus par l'aymant de l'aymée.

O gentil Ame estant tant estimée
Qui te pourra louer qu'en se taisant?
Car la parole est tousiours reprimée
Quand le subiet surmonte le disant.

[TEARS OF THE GREAT KING
UPON THE TOMB OF DONNA LAURA

Here, contained in small space, you may see
That which contains such great renown.
Pen, toil, language and duty
Were vanquished by the lover of the loved one.
O sweet soul, being held so dear,
Who can praise thee but by staying silent?
For speech is always repressed
When the subject surpasses the speaker.]

The simmering discontent of the citizens of Avignon against their Italian governors boiled over (not for the first time) in 1664. It was the outcome of a chain of events that had begun two years earlier when the French ambassador was being received at the Holy See. Laffi, for whom the events were of fairly recent date, glosses over certain key aspects of the story that would be embarrassing to an Italian Catholic.

The ambassador was, in fact, the victim of an apparently unpremeditated attack by the Vatican's Corsican Guard. Louis X I V responded immediately. The vice-legate of Avignon was ordered to remove the Italian garrisons from the city. The whole of the Comtat Venaissin and the papal state were then put under French administration. In 1664 a rapprochement was reached between the king and the Holy See, and Avignon and the rest of the County were ceded once more to Rome.

The new vice-legate, Alessandro Colonna, was a martinet who immediately introduced oppressive legislation that caused almost the whole population of Avignon to rise in revolt. The Italian garrison was chased out of the town and the papal palace, with Colonna in it, was besieged. He was forced, humiliatingly, to call on French troops to restore order. The leaders of the revolt were condemned to death, but had already fled. Instead, the house of one of their number was razed to the ground and a pyramid erected on the site, built from the rubble. It was to serve as a public warning to any future rebels. Its inscription named seven ringleaders and continued:

Many other gentlemen, emulating the king, also composed a variety of very good verses. It would take too long to repeat them here, so I shall pass them over.

After that we went to see the palace of Monsieur de Crillon. It has all been painted by our Bolognese artist, Master Matteo Borboni, and contains great riches and handsome furnishings. Next, we went to see the pyramid erected by the Pope's supporters, denouncing the rebels who rose up against Alexander V I I. They rebelled after the affront that the French ambassador received at Rome. This led to war between the king of France and the papal forces, though they subsequently concluded peace. On the pedestal of the pyramid is a record of the rebellion, which especially condemns its ringleaders. There is, moreover, a painting in the papal palace which depicts them as betrayers of their Prince. It gives their names and surnames, one being Gasparo, the other Tomaso Carleri.[b]

After seeing this, and some other worthwhile sights, we went back to the inn to get our bundles. Then, wearing our pilgrim's habit, we left by the 'bridge' gate, to go to Villeneuve. We went along the bridge, which is built entirely of white marble and is one of the finest in Christendom. From the middle you can see many villages in the distance. Further along you have to go down some steps to the river, because of the four broken arches, which I mentioned earlier. This was caused by the force of the water. Much harm has befallen some unfortunate people who have passed this way, because from this point you have to proceed by boat, and run great risks from the speed of the water. Having crossed the water and reached the other part of the bridge, we climbed up and entered the gates of Villeneuve. This is the first town in the old province of Gallia Narbonensis. Here, our bundles were examined by customs officers. The town belongs to the French king and has a great fortress built on high ground, overlooking the whole of Avignon. The town is all very solidly built.

After leaving this strongly fortified place we came to another town called Saint-Étienne. We were all the time travelling through country that was sometimes hilly, sometimes flat, though rather barren. We stopped here for the night. Next morning we continued to Sernhac, five leagues from Avignon, through a very pleasant, broad plain. We went to Bezouce, another league. The countryside here is

'Since they have escaped their well-deserved punishment, their effigies have been attached to a gibbet, their goods confiscated and the house of one of them destroyed ...' The hanging, conducted in absentia, took place in front of the papal palace.

The pyramid was demolished in 1768. It stood in what is now a little square, the Place de la Pyramide, which lies just off the rue Philonarde.

A The south of France had been the home of religious nonconformity since the twelfth century, and in the sixteenth the teachings of Calvin attracted a huge following. Whole regions of the Cévennes became solidly Huguenot. The civil war between Catholics and Protestants (1562-93) was followed by a royal decree, the Edict of Nantes, in 1598, granting various rights to the Huguenots, including that of fortifying and garrisoning their own towns. But it was not to last. Richelieu, who had come to power in 1624, was determined to suppress the military and political privileges of the Huguenots. In 1629 royal troops arrived in the Languedoc. Protestant strongholds in the mountainous Cévennes were besieged, captured and destroyed. In the same year the Peace of Alès set the seal on Richelieu's objectives, though the Huguenots retained the right to freedom of worship, which they had won at Nantes. In Laffi's day, although the movement remained numerically strong in the south of France, its influence in local affairs was gradually being eroded by the Catholic clergy.

flat, which makes the going very pleasant. Two leagues more and we reached Nîmes. We stopped here in order to see this beautiful and ancient city, even though it is full of heretics.[a]

On entering the city we went first to see the amphitheatre, the great monument built by the ancient Romans, which they call the Arena. It is all made of the finest marble, hardly at all disfigured by age, even though it is so old, because it is so highly regarded. It comprises the four orders:

B It is difficult today to distinguish the different classical orders of the arena.

C Nîmes was always a centre of religious dissent and had supported the Albigensians in the 12th and 13th centuries. In the second half of the 16th century during the Wars of Religion it was the scene of some of the worst fighting between Huguenot Protestants (who had established themselves in the city in 1532) and the Catholic authorities. Protestants were tried and burnt at the stake. A massacre of Catholics, known as the Michelade, occurred in 1568, following the feast day of St Michael (29 Sept.). The Consul and other Catholics were held prisoner in the house of a leading dissident, William the Hermit. The rising was quashed and its ringleaders condemned to death. The house of William the Hermit, in the street today called the rue des Greffes, was razed to the ground. On its site a pillar was erected, the 'monument' (mentioned by Laffi), which bore an inscription recording the events. The pillar had disappeared by the 19th century. It stood near the Town Hall, not the Palais de Justice.

Tuscan, Ionic, Doric and Corinthian, and is beautifully designed.[b] Inside, it is oval-shaped and there are flights of steps that go from top to bottom. There are wide passageways underneath, where they have set up inns, wine-shops and other kinds of stores. They sell many kinds of food here, such as you find in a town square. Then we were taken by some Catholics and heretics – who were all together! – to see the wolf that gave suck to Romulus and Remus. It is very old and is carved in *mezzo-rilievo* on one of the great columns that support the amphitheatre on the outside. It is well worth seeing. They took us to see the Palais de Justice, where there is a monument set up to mark the condemnation of heretics.[c]

From there they took us to see the temple of Diana. This temple is of great antiquity. It has three rectangular facades and a semicircular vault. There used to be an altar and a statue of the goddess. The orders are Corinthian and Composite, and the columns are of average height. They did not want us to go inside, as we did in the amphitheatre. From there we went to see the Capitol or, as it is sometimes

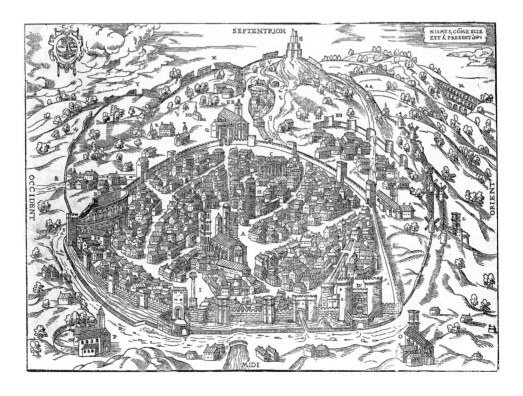

Today called the Maison Carrée. The temple of Diana (text on p. 61, fig. on p. 64) is now a ruin.

called, the house of the Empress Plautina.[a] It is very old and of average size, though not an exact square. The walls are of the finest marble, with pilasters that stand out round the outside. They are of the Corinthian order and support a big, magnificent entablature, which goes right round the house. The house itself has a single nave. The roof projects beyond the cornice in such a way that you cannot see how it is covered, unless you could climb above it. There is some splendid sculpture on the entablature. I have never seen better arabesques, they are excellent and much to be admired.

Throughout the city there are antiquities of many different kinds: monuments, statues, and similar things worth looking at. There is a spring near the temple of Diana – it has the same name, being nearby – which is a wonder to behold. In the evening, at sunset, it begins to seethe and goes on increasing so much that it boils right over, becoming very hot. After midnight it begins to diminish, continuing

B *The foaming water of the spring of
Nemausus (the spirit from whom
the city takes its name) can be
spectacular and sometimes dangerous to those living in the neighbourhood. Its rise and fall is
caused solely by rainfall and the
state of the rivers in the nearby
hills. It has nothing to do with the
time of day, nor do its waters boil.
Laffi may be confusing it with
one of the genuinely hot springs
– there are several in this region
of France.*

C *Not identified.*

─────

Fig. 21 *The city of Nîmes
attacked by Protestants in 1569.
(From Ménard, M., op. cit., vol. 5,
pl. facing p. 52.)*

─────

thus until sunrise. By then it has fallen so low that you cannot draw water except by using a rope. There are many
other curious things to be seen here but I omit them for the
sake of brevity.[b]

People enter and leave the city by one gate only, which
lies to the east. It is very fine. It is strongly fortified and
bears many ancient memorials to the emperors and other
famous men. There is a round bastion in front of the gate,
in the form of a ravelin, and there are deep moats and a covered walk-way. From Nîmes we went to Milhaud, a small
place one league away, where we lodged. Next morning we
continued to Uchaud, a large village, another league on.
Another two leagues took us to Lunel, a large, spacious and
populous village, once a town and still surrounded by a
wall. There is much coming and going here. It is very beautiful and lies in a plain, like all the other towns we have
passed through since leaving Avignon. From here we went
to Colombier,[c] two leagues from Lunel. On the way there
we met an Italian from Parma. He was on his way home
from Galicia. He told us how he had been attacked by a
band of robbers. They stripped him, took away his pieces
of eight, and assaulted him. Only his life was left to him,
and even that was shattered after they had beaten him. We
consoled him, gave him alms, and then went on our way.
We had not gone much more than a mile when we met two
solitary monks (or hermits) from Naples, who were also on
their way back from Galicia. They told us that they too
had been attacked in the border region between France
and Spain, beyond Perpignan. They were so maltreated
they went to the justices. Whereupon the magistrate sent
constables with them to the spot where the assault had occurred. On arrival they searched everywhere until they
found the three men, whom they bound and led back to the
city. They were immediately hanged and quartered, and
their quarters taken back to the place where they had committed the crime.

We questioned the monks about the road to Galicia and
they told us much. We gave them alms and also a letter to
take to Bologna, commending them to our relatives back
at home. Then they set off and we continued on our way,
very upset and anxious about the events they had related
to us. But we took courage, hoping for help from God and
St James, and continued on our way more cheerfully until

A *A surprising incident, in view of
the extent to which Protestant
activities had been curtailed in
Montpellier by the time of Laffi's
visit. Also, exceptionally for the
former Huguenot town, the main
fortifications, that is, the walls,
bastions and gates, still stood.
When the town fell to the army
of Louis XIII in 1622 after a
siege, only the external defences,
outside the walls, that had been
erected specially for the occasion,
were pulled down.*

we reached Colombier. This is a town which yields nothing, neither size, beauty nor any other thing, to Lunel.
From here we took the road to Montpellier, two long
leagues away. However, we covered them quickly because
it was quite flat and a good road. This is the best and most
fertile region in the whole of Gallia Narbonensis. When
we reached Montpellier the gatekeepers stopped us. They
asked us who we were, where we came from and where we
were going. When they learned that we were Italians and
Catholics, they – because they were heretics – refused absolutely to let us enter the city, saying no pilgrim had ever
been allowed in. They made it quite plain that we must stay
outside, and must be on our way next morning.[a]

So we turned back and found an inn, outside the city
walls, where we could lodge. Many local citizens came to
this inn to drink. Among them was a merchant from just
opposite who sold majolica. He was rather a good judge of
art and he and the landlord began to chat with us. My companion, the painter, produced some examples of his own
work. He also showed them many drawings of works by the
Carracci, Guido Reni, Raphael of Urbino, and other pictures by the best artists which, clearly, they liked very
much. We talked all that evening until supper time, and
they then ate in our company. When we told them how we

Laffi is here referring not to the great siege of 1622, but to events during the civil war in the second half of the previous century. The damage to the cathedral was more serious than he suggests. In 1567 one of the two towers at the west end was sapped and mined by the Huguenots. It fell on the nave, part of which collapsed. Part of the adjoining episcopal palace was also destroyed. Restoration work was begun about 1640, and would have been in progress during Laffi's visit.

Fig. 22 *The temple of Diana, Nîmes, as it appeared in the mid-18th century. (From Ménard, M., op. cit., vol. 7, pl. 1.)*

had not been allowed to enter the city, they promised to escort us next morning. They would take us through the whole city and show us the best sights.

After supper a group of youths and girls, who were taking an evening stroll in and around the town, gathered at the inn. They began to drink and soon became merry. Then they started to play a game which went like this: they formed themselves into a circle of about twelve, sometimes more, sometimes fewer, keeping the same distance from each other. Then they threw a big earthenware pot from one person to the next, round the circle. If anyone failed to catch it, letting it fall and break, he had to pay a forfeit. When the game was over we went to bed.

In the morning we rose and put on clothes suitable for the city. They came for us and took us inside by another gate. First we went to the cathedral to have the dimissory letter signed. It is a very big church and stands on high ground, dominating the whole city. It is on a little, round hill-top, with the rest of the town all round about. The church is badly damaged by cannon-shot. The heretics caused it when they rebelled in a sudden uprising in the city. They began to batter the place down, in particular attacking the church and the few Catholics who were still there. But by a miracle of God the cannon-balls, when they hit the wall, passed right through from one side to the other, leaving only a single hole the size of the ball and no bigger. It looked like a sieve, all perforated. Also, many balls were fired at the wall that never penetrated it at all. It was a miraculous thing to see. It was the same with the city walls to the north. It was on that side that the heretics' army was camped, and from where they attacked the city over several days. But seeing they were having no success, and that this was really by God's will, they called a truce with the Catholics. They then returned to the city and waited for the time that a new governor be appointed. These are all things that anyone passing this way can see for himself as I have done.[b]

The church, as I said, is a fine, very ancient building. On the high altar is a picture of St Peter causing the fall of Simon Magus. It was painted by Master Bourdon, a man of the highest ability in his art. The chapels are all orientated towards the high altar, as is not usually the case in Italy. In one of them is a painting begun by a Bolognese master,

A The large painting of the Fall of
Simon Magus by Sébastien Bourdon has survived and at present
hangs in the south transept. It
illustrates one of the best known
miracles of St Peter, to whom the
cathedral is dedicated. Bourdon,
a native of Montpellier and apparently a Protestant, painted it
in 1657. It probably symbolizes
the victory of Catholicism over
Protestantism. 'Father' here
denotes the bishop.

B What remains of the staff today
is preserved in the church of
St Roch at Montpellier. There are
well-attested documents in the
church archives which confirm
that it was the one that was shown
to Laffi. During the Revolution
it was thrown on a bonfire and
about two-thirds were burned
away. The seraph has gone. There
remain other marks, apparently
cut with the point of a sharp
knife, some of which are religious

which was left unfinished at his death. They wanted my
companion to stay and complete it, and would have given
him anything he asked for the work. As it is now very many
years since the painter died, the Father wanted no one else
to put his hand to it unless he thoroughly understood how
to paint in fresco on walls. He must also come from Bologna
so that he could imitate the style. They almost used force
to try and make us stay, because no other Bolognese had
passed that way, except us. But on no account would we
stay, for we had to continue our journey to Galicia. We did
promise, however, to help them on our return. The organ in
this church is more beautiful and more fantastical than any
I have seen in all my days.[a]

From here we went to the church of the Trinitarians to
say Mass. They keep a long stick here, which St Roch used
as a pilgrim's staff. No one may touch it except the clergy. It
is kept in a box which is just the right length and well protected with locks. Being a priest, I took it in my hands and
felt how heavy it was. The brother who showed it to me told
me it weighed twelve pounds. It has an iron ferrule at each
end and is slightly crooked. A seraph has been engraved on
a knot in the middle. It is of the usual length. No one knows
what kind of wood it is made of, though it has been seen by
many thousands of people.[b]

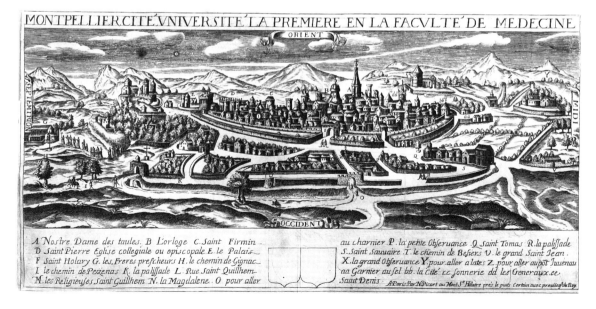

MONTPELLIER CITÉ VNIVERSITÉ LA PREMIÈRE EN LA FACVLTÉ DE MEDECINE

A Nostre Dame des taules. B L'orloge C. Saint Firmin.
D Saint Pierre Eglise collegiale ou episcopale E. le Palais
F Saint Holary G. les Freres prescheurs H. le chemin de Gignac
I le chemin de Pezenas K. la palissade L. Rue Saint Quillhem
M. les Religieuses Saint Guillhem N. la Magdalene . O pour aller

au charnier P. la petite Obseruance .Q. Saint Tomas R. la palissade
S. Saint Sauuaire .T. le chemin de Besiers U. le grand Saint Jean .
X. la grand Obseruance Y. pour aller a lates Z. pour aller au pot Juuenau
aa Garnier au sel bb. la Cité cc sonnerie dd les Generaux. ee
Saut Denis. A Paris Par N. Picart au Mont S.te Hilaire prés le puits Certain auec priuilege du Roy

the end, apparently made by nails, that would have held the ferrule in place.

There are good reasons to be-lieve that St Roch was a native of Montpellier, though somewhat more tenuous ones for supposing that the staff was his. He made one pilgrimage only, which was to Rome, and died on the return journey, having survived an attack of the plague. He was invoked by pilgrims as a protector against disease, especially the plague, and his image is still very widely seen along the roads to Compostella.

c *Episcopal.*

d *Not identified.*

Fig. 23 *Montpellier in the 17th century. A view from the West. (Bibliothèque Municipale, Montpellier.)*

Next, we went to see the royal[c] palace, which is still in the course of being rebuilt. It is decorated with splendid paintings. Then to another church, where they were saying an Office for the Dead.

We knelt before the altar together with our new ac-quaintances who were showing us round. We had been on our knees a little while, when a lady appeared and threw three *soldi* into my hat! This was extremely embarrassing, as we were in the company of our courteous friends, and to them it must have seemed that we were seeking alms. However, they told us that we must excuse her, for this was the lady's custom. Indeed, we noticed that she then made her way round the church, giving to all who were there, whether rich or poor. The rich, when they go out through the church door, pass it on to the poor who are standing outside, begging for alms.

In this church, as you will often find throughout France, there is a certain kind of wide bench with tall brackets fixed on it, for inserting large candles. There are many of them in a row along the benches. The candles are all made of red wax, indeed one sees very few white ones. They are all lighted at the Elevation of the Host and stay lit until the communion is done. When the service was over, we left the church and gave our three *soldi* to a poor man. There is also a fine university here. On our way out of the city we went down the street leading to our lodging house and took up our belongings.

Then we made for Gigean along a good road, all of it well surfaced. It runs through beautiful, flat country, filled with orchards, vines and olives, and every other kind of fruit tree. From Montpellier it is two leagues to Gigean, which we reached in the evening. It is a large town, circled by a wall. However, we did not stop here but continued on to a little village called Ruvirum.[d] This place is on a low hill, which extends into a great lake, like a peninsula. Next morning our road took us through many little hills, thick with vines and olives, to Loupian, two very long leagues, and then to St-Thibéry, another three leagues. Just before you arrive there you have to cross a small river, not very wide but dangerous. They have built a bridge over it many times, but in vain, for the river runs so fast it gets swept away. They have therefore provided a boat, so that car-riages, carts, animals and passengers can cross. It is a public

A This refers to the remains of a Roman bridge across the River Hérault near St-Thibéry. The central arches fell long ago. Four, on the south side are still standing. So far as is known no attempt has ever been made to restore it.

B None of the fortifications described by Laffi is now standing though parts of the old wall are still extant to the south-west of the city. The gate with the king's statue was the former Porte des Carmes, which was situated at the east end of the present Rue du 4 Septembre. Many public statues of members of the ancien régime were destroyed during the Revolution. The 'huge bastion on the left' was the wall of the old citadel. The pilgrims' hospice adjoined the citadel and stood in the present place Jean Jaurès.

crossing and the mail-coach goes this way, so they make a big charge for the hire of the boat. The revenue goes to the queen of France. For this reason they will never build the bridge again, because there is a good profit to be made.[a]

Having crossed over, we came to St-Thibéry, which is only the distance of a musket-shot. It is a fine place, well-fortified and surrounded by a wall. It is a big town and has splendid buildings and a great square, where they sell quantities of fruit. On leaving, we made for Béziers, three very long leagues away. Before we got there, there was a long hill to climb and here we met a poor Roman. He told us that he too was going to Santiago in Galicia, so we walked together, happy to have found a companion on such a long journey. And so, chatting with each other about out own home towns, we arrived at Béziers in the evening.

It is a big city, standing on a hill, not very high, and is very beautiful. It makes a fine view from a distance, because of its many towers and campaniles. You enter through a big new gate at the east. On your left is a huge bastion, built of masonry. The gatehouse itself is very fine, bearing the coat of arms and a statue of Louis XIV, and has lovely finishing touches. On entering you come to a great square, clean and uncluttered, because there is another one for the fruit and vegetable market. This one is used only as a parade ground. There are a number of large religious houses including one for nuns. By the gate, on your left, is a large hospice that provides lodging and other charity for pilgrims. The clergy are cared for separately and are treated lavishly. For the rest they provide only bread and wine, unlike monks whom they also treat well. We left our Roman companion here and went to a supper-house, where the landlord also had rooms to let.[b]

Just as we were leaving in the morning we met a priest who asked us where we came from. We told him we were Italians from Bologna and were going to Galicia. He said he had been to Rome and spoke good Italian. He asked what skills my companion had and the latter replied that he was a painter. The priest was delighted to hear this. He showed us much kindness, inviting us to take a meal with him. This was so that he could have his portrait painted. My companion pointed out that he had no materials with him, but the priest replied that he would be happy if it could simply be done in *lapis rosso*, that is, 'sanguine', or red chalk.

The scudo *– a 'shield', that is, a coin depicting the arms of the issuing authority – was either gold or silver. The latter was known as the white scudo, in Italy* scudo bianco, *in France* écu blanc (cublanc *according to Laffi).*

D *The present Pont-Vieux over the Orb.*

E *The Aude.*

F *Laffi is describing correctly, if somewhat disjointedly, part of the Canal du Midi, which was in the course of construction when he went that way. The idea of building a waterway that linked the Atlantic with the Mediterranean was first conceived by the Romans but was only finally achieved in the seventeenth century. The Canal du Midi, or Canal du Languedoc, as it was formerly called, connects the Mediterranean with Toulouse where it joins other waterways to the Atlantic. It has 103 locks. Capestang lies beside one of the longest reaches, of some thirty-four miles. This section is fed by the river Cesse, which Laffi crossed. The river was diverted through a specially constructed channel, as he mentions. The aqueduct allows the excess waters of the Cesse to pass under the canal.*

So he did it, in two hours, at the priest's house. When it was finished he gave us an excellent meal and a silver *scudo* which they call a *cublanc.*[e]

When you leave this town you cross a splendid bridge over a broad river,[d] that runs outside the city to the west. It flows through a wide and pleasant plain, full of orchards and market-gardens. There are some beautiful mansions and broad fields with olives and many vines. The country-side is truly beautiful, growing every kind of fruit and cereals. So we made our way to Narbonne, four leagues from Béziers. Half way along this stretch of road you come to a wide river which you cross by boat.[e] On the river bank is a walled town called Capestang. Here the river flows into a canal they are making. When finished it will go from one sea to the other, through the Languedoc. It is a considerable undertaking. At this point they have made an aqueduct and protected the canal with high walls. It has many locks. They have dug for a distance of a mile in order to channel the river.[f] From Capestang we continued our journey as far as Narbonne.

Fig. 24 *The Béziers gate at Narbonne, also known as the Porte Royale, in the first half of the 19th century. (Courtesy of the Archives Municipales, Narbonne.)*

A *Narbonne was well defended from the time of its foundation by the Gauls in the seventh century* B C. *A Greek historian writing about* 500 B C *described it as 'a town surrounded by massive walls that are constructed of huge blocks of stone' (in* Periodos Ges *[Travels round the Earth], attributed to Hecatæus of Miletus,* fl. *6th-5th century* B C *). For many centuries it was the capital city of the region under various rulers. By the eighth century* A D *its walls had been destroyed and rebuilt by Romans, Visigoths, Saracens and Franks. The walls were again seriously damaged by the English during the Hundred Years' War and subsequently restored at great cost to the citizens. In* 1510 *a new wall, built outside the medieval wall that was mainly still standing, was begun by Louis* X I I. *It embodied new architectural features, such as the ravelin, that reflected the latest*

6

THROUGH LANGUEDOC
Narbonne to Toulouse

WHEN WE REACHED NARBONNE THEY asked us what country we were from and where we were going. We told them we were Italians and on our way to Galicia so they let us in. At the entrance to the town you are confronted by a high and strong wall with very substantial bastions and ravelins, their walls all faced with masonry. There is a covered-way all round with a strong palisade. We entered the ravelin by way of a long bridge over the moat. Here there is a strong garrison where they asked our names, surnames and nationality. We were then allowed to cross another bridge that leads from the ravelin to the city gate itself. It is very fine, made of white marble and has ancient inscriptions. The gate is very strong with portcullises and drawbridges. The last one, on the in-side, is raised and lowered by a winch that is operated by a great wheel – a splendid sight.[a]

Once inside the city we went directly to the main square. The streets are very narrow but full of shops and crowded with people. We stood for a while in the square, admiring it, because it is so fine, even though it is quite small. Then we went in the direction of the harbour. It is first-rate and always full of merchant ships. They come and go along the great river that flows into the Mediterranean.[b]

We walked around the town to look at the many mon-asteries and churches. They have some fine paintings by accomplished artists, especially at the Capuchins – who have a splendid picture by Bassano.[c]

The large monasteries are generous alms-givers to pil-grims. They also have good hospices. Whoever wishes to lodge there has to apply to the 'Consul', the local magis-trate, as did our companion from Rome. The Consul makes out a form, sealed with his own hand, which you present to

house was closed following the Revolution. Bassano was the name taken by a family of Venetian painters, properly called da Ponte. The Musée d'Art et d'Histoire at Narbonne holds an Adoration of the Magi by Leandro da Ponte (1558-1623) and an Adoration of the Shepherds by his father Jacopo (1510-92), who was the most talented member of the family. The former painting was not in Narbonne in Laffi's day. The provenance of the latter is uncertain but could have been the one he saw.

A *In the early part of Chap. 1 (not included in this translation) Laffi nominates Bologna university (his* alma mater*) as the finest 'among all the sixty-six that there are in the world' – which he then enumerates.*

B *The chasuble.*

C *The largest church in that city.*

D *The palace has two spiral staircases, neither of which corresponds to Laffi's description: a simple circular spiral with a conventional newel-post of the type commonly found in church towers (1290-1311); and a so-called 'Grand Staircase' (1628) of masonry, rectangular, with rising balustrades round a central well and supported by eight piers. It served the archbishop's private apartments.*

the overseer of the hospice. He then leads you inside and allots you a good bed.

This town is large and very grand. It is very old and is surrounded by strong, high walls of white marble, of which there is a plentiful supply in these parts. It lies in a broad plain where there are the most magnificent châteaux, old and new, with splendid fountains that spout great jets of water. There are two squares where they sell all kinds of vegetables, fruit and also fish. It is plentiful and cheap. There is also a university, the most thriving of all the sixty-six mentioned above.[a] By the time we had walked all round the city, it was evening so we went back to the inn.

Next morning we went to the bishop's palace to have the dimissory signed. He made us wait a short while, then having signed it, gave us alms for the Mass. Then we went down to the cathedral, but the sacristan would not let us say Mass because we were not wearing the long vestment.[b] Instead, he too gave us alms for the Mass, saying we should go to one of the monasteries where we could say Mass dressed as we were. We left the cathedral by the door of the episcopal palace, which is a very tall building like San Petronio in Bologna.[c] The bishop's palace adjoins the cathedral in such a way that it appears to be all one building. Being so large it can be seen from many leagues away. It has a great oval spiral staircase, all of masonry, which goes from bottom to top of the palace. In the well of the staircase are two tall, thick columns extending right up from the base and supporting a great vaulted ceiling.[d]

The building is very old, displaying several orders of architecture, all in white marble inside and out, like the fabric of the cathedral. The latter has many very old inscriptions showing that the city was powerful before and after the Roman era. When we left the cathedral we went to the Carmelites to say Mass. Then we took up our belongings and went straight away to the hospice to collect our Roman companion who was waiting for us, as he had said. He too picked up his bundle and so we set off from Narbonne for Villedaigne, two leagues on. We left by the west gate along a good, broad road, quite flat for a long way. Here there is a very old aqueduct built by the Romans when they governed this region. It runs beside the road for about two leagues. It draws its water from a river running through the district. In order to build it they had to bore

E *Vestiges of an aqueduct, probably Roman, possibly medieval, have been traced in the communes of Névian-Montredon, to the west of Narbonne, through which Laffi passed. It is not known whether it supplied water to Narbonne itself, though this seems likely.*

As for vinegar, Greek and Latin writers mention its use to make rock friable. Laffi may have had in mind a description by Livy (Bk 21, ch. 37) of Hannibal crossing the Alps. On reaching an impassable cliff 'it was necessary to cut through the rocks. They therefore felled and lopped a number of large trees which grew around and made a huge pile of timber. As soon as a wind arose, strong enough to excite the flames, they set fire to it. They then poured vinegar on to the heated stones to render them soft and crumbling, and with iron implements opened a way through the rock thus heated by the fire.' See further: Frassinetti, P., 'L'aceto di Annibale', Giornale Italiano di Filologia, Naples, 1950, fascicle 3, pp. 200-205.

through many hills, not very high, but of solid rock. A way was cut right through them with the use of fire, iron bars, vinegar and chisel. The aqueduct brings an ample supply of water to Narbonne, which would otherwise have to rely on the river for drinking-water which, being near the sea, is somewhat salty and always turbid because of the ebb and flow of the tide.[e]

We continued on our way beside the aqueduct for about two leagues until we came to Villedaigne. Before entering the town you have to be ferried across a wide river – the same from which the aqueduct takes its water. We were taken across without paying anything. On reaching the other side the boatman asked us if we would like to eat at his inn because, from there onwards for a good stretch, there was neither house nor hostelry. So we stopped as it was nearly midday. The man prepared us a salad and nothing else, which cost us six sous and another ten sous for the wine. This was the kindness he did us having ferried us over for nothing!

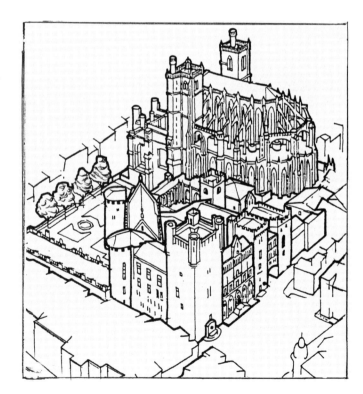

Fig. 25 *An artist's impression of the archiepiscopal complex, Narbonne. The buildings that form the archbishops' palace are in the foreground; behind them is the cathedral. (Courtesy of the Archives Municipales, Narbonne.)*

73

Our appetites having thus been whetted, though far from satisfied we set off for Lézignan, three leagues away across a wide plain. Here a terrible wind struck us, so much so we could hardly move. We walked in ditches as best we could and had to tie our hats on our heads or the wind would have carried them away. We walked all day in that wind, which blew on our stomachs and was very cold. At last, in the evening, we reached Lézignan. It is a large place and is encircled by a double ring of walls, one so close to the other that there is scarcely room for a man to pass between them. On the outside there is a ditch and a counter-ditch, both full of water. We went a short way into the town, but as it was now late we asked a Franciscan Observantine where there might be good lodgings. He said good lodgings were to be had but living was dear inside the town. We should do better outside, in the suburban quarter, where one paid less and, moreover, it would be more convenient for us if we wanted to be on our way early because the gates opened late. We followed his advice and went outside the town to the White Horse inn, where we lodged in comfort. But it cost us dear for I believe this town is the very house and home of shortages. I shall not speak of the bread and wine – dearer than a brother – I will mention only one thing to prove the truth of what I am saying: a dish of trotters (which the Florentines call *peducci*), which is merely four lambs' trotters from the knee down, cost us twenty French sous, the same as forty of our *soldi*!

There were two French pilgrims here who were going to Rome. One of them played the violin and spoke Latin, very badly, to my companion. He uttered the grossest solecisms and his violin-playing was equally outlandish. He tried to persuade us that he played very well indeed. He was going to Italy, in particular to Rome, where he would have great success since no one played the instrument so well as he. He flattered himself that he was the greatest player in those parts. To test him we made him play the whole night, with the result that the innkeeper could get no sleep. But he was clumsy and dull-witted and accompanied his playing with such grimaces and cries and shouts that he seemed more like an animal.

Thus we passed the night, and early next morning we set off for Carcassonne, three leagues away. Once again we were troubled by the wind, only it was worse than before,

The stone bridge, today called the Pont Vieux, spans the River Aude and connects the citadel (La Cité) to the lower town. It was built when the lower town was founded in 1247 by Louis IX. The market square is the present day Place Carnot, formerly the Place aux Herbes, which is situated in the middle of the lower town. The porticoed food market was pulled down in the eighteenth century.

B *The citadel is one of the most remarkable medieval fortified towns to have survived today. The rocky spur on which it stands was a settlement in the sixth century B C and was fortified by the Romans between 43 and 30 B C. The present inner wall corresponds to a ring of ramparts raised by the Romans against Barbarian invaders in the third century A D. Louis I X was responsible for building the outer defensive wall. After the citadel had been allowed to decay for some two centuries the French government in 1850 decreed that the fortifications be demolished. The decree was overturned and a great programme of restoration was thereupon undertaken by the French architect, Viollet-le-Duc. Several kinds of stonework can be distinguished, according to the date of construction.*

C *The Aude.*

so we walked in ditches, each of us on our own, behind their banks of earth. We carried on in this way until midday, not realising we had lost our companion. He had found his way through some hills and had come to a walled place called Capendu where he stopped for dinner, thinking he would meet us there. But then he left, asking the way to Carcassonne. I and our Roman companion took a different way. We came to a small place where folk were at dinner. They would take no payment from us, indeed on our departing they gave us a cheese and two large loaves, asking us to pray to God for them. Finally, on leaving we asked them the way to Carcassonne which they kindly showed us. We walked all day through many fields and open country, all cultivated and having an abundance of the very best wheat. Late in the evening we reached Carcassonne.

This is the first town you come to in the province of Languedoc. And there, as we looked ahead, we saw our companion sitting on the bridge. Joyfully we ran to embrace him, for both he and we had been in very low spirits all that day. We went to the inn that he had found, telling each other about our travels. Next morning we walked around Carcassonne. It is a powerful, rich, trading city. Everywhere is so packed with shops that I have never before seen so many together in all my days, and all so well arranged. There is a big, splendid square where all one's daily wants can be obtained in plenty. In the middle is a large building with porticoes, exactly square, where the grain and vegetable markets are held. The dry measures for the grain are hewn from stone. Above is the public granary.[a]

Returning from our walk we found ourselves outside the east gate where we had entered the previous evening. This suburban area is wide, long and exceedingly fine. To the south, rising above it, is a strong citadel, indeed a fortress, which is so big that, seen from a distance, it looks like a city itself. It is a fine sight. It is surrounded by a double ring of defensive walls, the first of which is as high as the other. The outer wall has round bastions at intervals. The inner wall, quite close to it, is very high and has high, fortified towers, roofed with a dome. It all makes a splendid sight. The walls are built of masonry.[b]

Between the lower town and the suburbs flows a broad river,[c] spanned by a long and splendid bridge. On the other side lies another outer district encircled by walls and a moat

The Canal du Midi.

with strong bastions and drawbridges at the gates. Here you enter the main town, fortified with walls and bastions and a moat. After walking round the town for a while, we left by the gate that leads to Castelnaudary, some five leagues from Carcassonne. After two leagues we came across several hundred people working on the great canal.[a] They had started from Toulouse and had now reached this point, a distance of seventeen leagues. We walked beside the canal for a few leagues, but then left it because it does not always run alongside the public road, having to turn this way or that according to the lie of the land. We carried on to Castelnaudary passing three pretty villages on the way.

It is a large place with all the feeling of a city. It stands on the top of a little hill and can therefore be seen from afar. It is very long, as you can see from its outline. In it there are many churches with high bell-towers which made a beautiful sight from a distance. It has a defensive wall with many fortified round towers, also a few square ones. There are in addition, outside the town but still on the hill, some twenty windmills, half on one side of the town, half on the other. They make a very charming sight.

'Qui fabricano navi per il nuovo canale, perché qui si ritorna a caminarvi dietro.' The meaning is not quite clear. It seems to suggest that the building of the canal had by then only reached this point.

———

Fig. 26 *The citadel, Carcassonne, showing the double row of walls. The space between them served as lists, or jousting-ground. Early 20th century. (Courtesy of the Director of Archives, Aude.)*

———

A great deal of traffic goes through the town as it lies between Carcassonne and Toulouse. In this neighbourhood, as in the other villages between Toulouse and Carcassonne, there are vast numbers of poultry and geese. One sees whole flocks of them, in their thousands, with their keepers, like shepherds with sheep. They go from one village to another, staying out in the fields both day and night. Sometimes they are spread over a whole stretch of land, particularly if there are two or three flocks together, and the ground then seems covered in black or, if they are geese, white. We often thought we were looking at a whole lot of washing laid out to dry, which turned out to be geese when we got nearer. There are usually three or four people looking after a flock, more or fewer according to its size.

We stayed the night in the town and in the morning went to the principal church. We were not able to say Mass but, instead, they gave us alms and told us to go to the Carmelites. There, we said Mass and gave communion to many people as it was Pentecost. When Mass was over, as we were leaving the altar still vested and carrying the chalice, they asked us to go round the tombs, saying the *De Profundis* and other prayers for the dead. We went round many tombs in this fashion, accompanied by the owners, all of whom gave alms. I believe that, what with the alms for the Mass and what they gave me going round the tombs, I made a whole *scudo*.

Next we went to Villefranche, three very long leagues away and then followed the road through Villenouvelle to Baziège, another four leagues. Here we spent the night, which cost us a lot, everything being very dear. Next morning we said Mass at the Observantines and also went round the tombs, as on the day before. But we picked up very little from it on account of local poverty. We made off without delay to escape a place that was so poor in possessions, so rich in hunger. Next we came to Montgiscard, another two leagues. Here they build ships for the new canal, because here they turn round to go back the way they came.[b] There are many locks, drawbridges and other stone buildings on the canal. This great undertaking, promoted by the king of France, is to join the two seas, the Ocean and the Mediterranean, and is capable of taking any merchant vessel whatever. We walked alongside it for three leagues, which took us from Montgiscard to Toulouse.

TOULOUSE TO RONCESVALLES

7

GASCONY & THE PYRENEES

Toulouse to Roncesvalles

A *The 'east gate' by which Laffi entered the city was the former Porte St-Michel. It led across a court to an inner gate, the Porte du Château and thence to the present Grande Rue St-Michel.*

B *St-Étienne.*

Fig. 27 *St-Sernin, Toulouse, west-front.*

Y OU CAN SEE TOULOUSE WHEN YOU ARE still three leagues away. It lies in a broad, very fertile plain and is a really wonderful, magnificent sight. Before entering the city you come to a large suburban district, and many more after that, which almost form another city in themselves. All of this lies outside the east gate, where you enter the town. We passed through the outer districts and came to a gate with a drawbridge that was overlooked by a round bastion. This was so big that there are many dwelling-places inside it. You enter the town through this bastion and across another drawbridge.[a]

When we entered we went a long way to find an inn, because it was so late. Early next morning we made our way to the cathedral[b] to have the dimissory signed. However, the vicar general was in the choir saying the office so we waited until he had finished. Meanwhile we looked round the church, which is large, very old and beautiful. It has an organ, its size beyond measure and finely wrought. There are many very old paintings and sculptures. When the service was over we went straight to the vicar who courteously signed the dimissory. From here we went to the Novitiates' College of the Jesuit Fathers to make confession, because we had been told that there was a father there who spoke Italian very well. We found him and he confessed us with kindness and courtesy. After that we went to the Benedictine Fathers to say Mass, where I gave communion to my companion. Having concluded our devotions we went around the town. We saw many monasteries and churches, which are very delightful, especially the principal church, St-Sernin. It is big and very, very old and has so many relics and remains of saints it would be quite an undertaking to mention them all. There are the bodies of St James the

A St-Sernin is one of a series of great
Romanesque 'pilgrimage' churches
and was begun in the second half
of the eleventh century. It is strik-
ingly similar to Compostella cathedral in its architecture and in
certain items of sculpture. It is
recognised that one must have
served as the model for the other,
St-Sernin probably being the
earlier. The famous relics, housed
in ambulatory chapels and in an
upper and lower crypt, were once
even more numerous than they are
today. Pilgrims still make what
used to be called a 'tour of the

holy bodies' round the east end of
the church. Laffi makes a curious
slip in his list of saints: Thaddæus and Jude are the same person.

B The 'great gallery' (gran ter-
razzo) is presumably the trifor-
ium, which extends all round the
church except for the east end. It
has windows at regular intervals.
The 'facade' (volto) must surely
refer to the west front of the
church, which has five windows
above the portals that would have
made excellent strongpoints for

the defenders. The artillery, of
fairly small calibre, was installed
in 1562 as part of the defence
against Protestants who, as Laffi
observes, were finally expelled
from the city. This date marked
the beginning of over thirty years
of almost continuous civil war in
France between Catholics and
Huguenot Protestants. In Laffi's
day the power of Protestantism
was greatly diminished. The Edict
of Nantes (1598) which had guar-
anteed them freedom of worship
and other rights was revoked in
his lifetime in 1685.

Fig. 28 *Louis XIII and his
retinue entering Toulouse in 1632.
The outer gate, the Porte
St-Michel, is on the left; the inner
gate, the Porte du Château, is on
the right. This was the 'East Gate'
by which Laffi entered. (Archives
Municipales, Toulouse: Annales
manuscrites, Livre VI,
chronique 304.)*

———

Fig. 29 *Toulouse in 1631.
The Porte St-Michel is on the
far right. (Musée Paul Dupuy;
photograph AMP, Toulouse.)*

Less, St Matthew, St Thaddæus, ss Simon and Jude, and
St Barnabas the apostle. They are kept in silver caskets and
make a profoundly wonderful sight. The choir is old and
entirely done in mosaic, where the canons go in a fine and
solemn procession, something truly worth seeing.[a]

Above the facade is a great gallery with big windows that
face outwards. At the windows there are artillery pieces,
one at each. They were put there by the Catholics when
they drove the heretics from the town. The place is now
free of this plague because the Catholics absolutely refuse
to allow them in. They have to live in the outer districts and
in the villages.[b]

We left the city, crossing over a great bridge which is entirely of marble and is the finest and the broadest I have

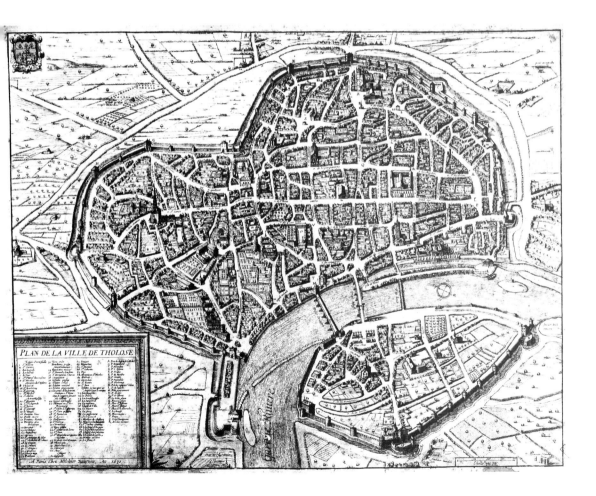

PLAN DE LA VILLE DE THOLOSE.

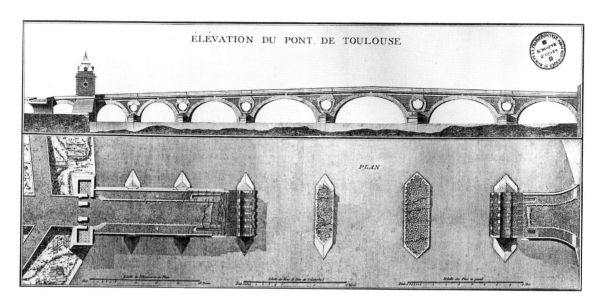

ÉLÉVATION DU PONT DE TOULOUSE

PLAN

The Pont Neuf was begun in 1602 and was remarkable in design and construction. The triumphal arch, erected at the western end, was designed by Lemercier, the architect of Louis XIII (1601-43). The king's equestrian statue was carved in bas-relief above the centre of the archway. The inscription (mentioning his successor, Louis XIV) was authorized by the city magistrates in 1667 in honour of a newly appointed governor of the province, the Duke of Verneuil. He was the natural son of Henry IV, and therefore half-brother of Louis XIII. The inscription seems to have been simply a gesture of loyalty to the monarchy. The two statues were placed in niches on the arch in 1662 to celebrate the centenary of the defeat of the Toulousan Huguenots. One represented Christ, the other the Virgin trampling on the figure of Heresy personified. The arch was dismantled between 1858 and

ever seen. I did not measure its length because it is so long, but out of curiosity I measured the width. It is twenty-eight paces and is divided into three lanes; the one in the middle is for carts, carriages and other wheeled traffic, the other two on either side, which are higher than the roadway, are for the gentry. It is a marvellous structure, not simply because it is made of marble, but it is so flat that you go neither up one side nor down the other. A stranger, crossing it in the dark, would not realise, unless he had been told, that he was going over a bridge at all.[a]

The bridge spans a great, navigable river, the Garonne, which divides Languedoc from Gascony. At one end is a large gateway or, one should say, a triumphal arch that bears an inscription dedicated to King Louis and his coat of arms. There is also an equestrian statue of the king, all in white marble. The whole thing is a superb sight, not only for the marble but for its architecture and ornamentation. But I will pass that over in order not to weary you too much – and it would be too much effort for me! I will just tell you about the inscription which is below the king's statue in the middle of the triumphal arch. It commemorates the king's conquest of Toulouse and his having the bridge built, an undertaking worthy of so great a monarch. I thought it right to set it out just as it appears on the arch, word for word, thus:

FACE DE L'ARC DE TRIOMPHE VERS LA VILLE, ET PROFIL DE LA GRANDE ARCHE.

Fig. 30-31 *The Pont Neuf, Toulouse, from an engraving of 1783:* (left) *elevation;* (right) *the triumphal arch, showing the equestrian statue of Louis* XIII. *(Courtesy of the Archives Municipales, Toulouse.)*

1867 to allow room for increasing traffic. The statues are today in the Musée des Augustins.

B *James Hogarth writes: The inscription, in rather clumsy hexameters, has some obvious errors of transcription (either Laffi's, or more likely a printer misreading his handwriting).* Saluti *should be* Salutis; perimusque *means nothing and is probably a misprint for* primusque; iugens *is a misreading of* iugans; *and* disperatumque *should be* desperatumque.

ANNO RESTAURATIONIS SALUTI
MDCLXVIII [b]
Qui dedit Oceano, docuit te dulce GARUMNA
ferre iugum, perimusque tuas compescuit undas,
hactenus inviso iugens tua littora ponte;
hoc opus inceptum, disperatumque pependit,
donec LUDOVEUM *foelicia secla tulerunt,*
qui tota solus posset mirante TOLOSA:
tantum indignanti cervici imponere molem.

[IN THE YEAR OF OUR LORD,
1668
He who put a yoke on the ocean taught thee too,
O Garonne, to bear a sweet yoke and was the first to
constrain thy waters, linking thy two banks by a
bridge, up to now unseen. The work was begun but
remained in suspense, despaired of, until a fortunate
age brought Louis, who alone was able, with all
Toulouse wondering, to impose such a great mass
on thy impatient neck.]

Not far from the bridge, on the river bank, is a small chapel dedicated to the patriarch, St Dominic. It commemorates a miracle which happened here when he saved from drowning many pilgrims who were returning from St James in Galicia. The boat in which they were crossing the river overturned because the waters were in spate (for at that time

TOULOUSE TO RONCESVALLES

there was no bridge). We then went to see the Dominican monastery,[a] a fine, ancient place. It was the first monastery founded by the glorious St Dominic in the time of Innocent III. The Order was confirmed by Honorius III in 1216. Dominic stayed in Toulouse for many years, converting thousands of souls, restoring the dead to life and performing countless other miracles, not only in this city but all over France, Italy and Spain. Dominic was born in Spain in 1170 in the time of [Pope] Alexander III and the Holy Roman Emperor Frederick I [Barbarossa]. It was during the reign of Alfonso IX of Castile, who defeated Miramolin at Tolosa in an unforgettable battle.[b]

Dominic was born at Calaruega into the eminent family of Guzmán, which marked him out for a great future in both sanctity and learning. His mother dreamed she gave birth to a dog with a burning brand in its mouth, which had come to light up the world's spiritual darkness. In another dream, when he was only new-born, bees dripped ambrosial honey on his lips with which he would nourish the holy faith by word and deed. He indeed became a new Atlas while above his head was seen a star that illuminated the whole universe. After having inspired many followers who, in their turn, shouldered his great burden he passed from this life to one that is eternal and blessed, to enjoy the just reward for his glorious deeds, in Bologna on the 5th August, 1223, in the reign of Frederick II. He was canonized in the following year by Pope Gregory IX.[c]

The monastery's church, which we saw next, is old and very beautiful. They have many relics besides the human remains of saints. In particular, St Thomas Aquinas lies here, in a most sumptuous chapel whose architecture can only be described at great length. That seems to me a very difficult task. Suffice to say that the glorious body of the 'Angelic Doctor' lies here, he who was famous throughout the world. He was called angelic because his way of life was like an angel's, because of the acuteness of his writings and his clarifications of the most obscure passages of Holy Scripture, and because the virginal purity that he maintained on earth was equal to that of an angel in heaven.

This 'dumb ox', as he was sometimes known, bellowed so loud he thundered throughout the whole world. He wrote so heroically of the deeds of Jesus of Nazareth that it would not have been surprising if Jesus had said to him, *Bene scrip-*

Fig. 32 *Painting by F. Traini of St Dominic rescuing pilgrims from drowning in the Garonne at Toulouse. (Nat. Galleria, Pisa.)*

A *The Dominicans were known as
Jacobins in France because their
first house, in the north, was established in the rue St-Jacques in Paris
in 1218. They had already been
installed in Toulouse in 1215, the
present monastery being built between about 1230 and 1340. It
underwent many later refurbish-
ments.*

A *The Dominicans were known as
Jacobins in France because their
first house, in the north, was established in the rue St-Jacques in Paris
in 1218. They had already been
installed in Toulouse in 1215, the
present monastery being built between about 1230 and 1340. It
underwent many later refurbish-
ments.*

*In 1369 the remains of Thomas
Aquinas, who had recently been
canonized, were brought from
Italy to Toulouse on the orders
of Pope Urban V, the last pope
but one to reign on French soil at
Avignon. They were installed in
the Jacobins' church. Between
1623 and 1626 a splendid edifice,
a veritable mausoleum, was built
to enshrine the saint's remains.
They lay in a coffin of wrought
gold and silver. This was the tomb
that Laffi saw. It was destroyed in
the first years of the Revolution,
though the relics were moved for
safety to St-Sernin in 1791. They
were restored to the Jacobins'
church in 1974 where they lie in
a modest coffin of gilded wood
which dates from 1827.*

*Laffi would have known the
Golden Legend (1255-66),
which tells of a hermit who
prophesied to Thomas's mother,
when she had barely conceived,
that her child was destined for
greatness. It also tells how his
death was foretold by the miraculous appearance of a star.*

B *'violone'.*

sisti de me Thoma [you have written well of me, Thomas]. He set out to emulate in all things the life of his great spiritual father, Dominic. He seemed, just like Dominic, to have a shining star above his head. He was laden with virtues throughout his life, as was foretold before his birth. Reaching his last hour this new swan, uttering its sacred song, turned away, with its much extolled virtues, to make the journey from this earth to heaven on the 7 March 1274. He performed miracles in this life, in death and after death.[a]

We left the church and went into the other half of the town. This is situated in the province of Gascony, where they dress, speak and live in the Gascon manner. They have their own vicar and separate cathedral. We took a walk round the whole town. It is somewhat smaller than Bologna and is very fine and thronging with people. It is a famous seat of learning, having one of the sixty-six universities I mentioned previously. It is well stocked with the good blood of gentlefolk. The city has a regional assembly which supervises the whole of Languedoc. It was now growing late so we went to our lodgings. Next morning we took up our belongings and went back to the cathedral to obtain our indulgence. As we left the cathedral we met a priest who was taking the Host to someone who was sick, so we accompanied him as far as the sick man's house. Then we made our way to the hospice to fetch our Roman companion and so left the city.

Outside the gate there is a large, very fine suburban district with many workshops where they make sewing needles. We went into one of them to see the kind of skills required to manufacture them. There is a large wooden wheel which drives a smaller one made of stone. A craftsman sits in front of it and takes a small bundle of needles to sharpen them against the stone wheel. On touching the wheel the needles give off a great flame. Therefore the craftsman, to avoid getting hurt and to see what he is doing, wears an iron mask with glass eye-holes. He likewise wears an iron breast-plate and gauntlets, otherwise his clothes and his face would be burned. It all makes such a noise and din that it can be heard a mile away. The ropes that go round the wheel are as thick as the ones used by bell-ringers to ring the bass bell or, as we might say, a double-bass[b] – and are made of the same material.

We left the workshop and made our way over an always very fair and fertile plain until we reached L'Isle Jourdain, a town a good four leagues away. It is a small place but pleasant, though we did not stop here but went straight through, continuing to Gimont, about another two leagues. It is quite a large town but practically uninhabited. We

Fig. 33 *The mausoleum of St Thomas Aquinas seen from the east. It had four sides, all equally ornate and each with an altar. The reliquary chest stands in the centre. The effigy at the top represents St Thomas. (From Wolff, P,* Histoire de Toulouse, *1978. Courtesy Édouard Privat.)*

A The Cistercian abbey at Gimont,
called Planselve, was founded in
the middle of the twelfth century
and was known for its hospitality
towards Compostellan pilgrims.
Its remains lie among meadows a
mile or so from the town, beside
the River Gimone. The complex
of monastic buildings, some of
which are still standing, covered a
huge area and included several
windmills. The abbey was able to
provide everything within its own
walls for the livelihood of the
monks. It was closed in 1802 by
the Revolution, when the church
and some other buildings were
pulled down.

B The choir-stalls and windows are
justly famous works of art of the
French Renaissance. The former
took some fifty years to accom-
plish, between 1500 and 1552.
There are one hundred and thirteen stalls in two tiers. They are
carved in oak (not walnut) and
represent scenes from the Old and
New Testaments, the figures of
prophets, sibyls, evangelists,
Church Fathers and personified
virtues. Taken as a whole they

stayed the night here, doing better than we expected in
such a deserted place, for we found it well provisioned. In
the morning we went to say Mass at St Bernard's monastery, where the sacristan gave us breakfast.[a]

After that we went on to Aubiet, two leagues on. It is a
beautiful, agreeable town but full of heretics. So then we
walked three leagues without a break until we reached
Auch. Auch is the first city of the province of Aquitaine,
but when we arrived it was evening so that we had hardly
entered the city before they closed the gates. In the morning we went to the cathedral to say Mass but we had to wait
a little until High Mass was finished, after which they feed
the pilgrims. After our Mass we went briefly round the
church, while our companion went to eat with the other pilgrims. Their meal had been prepared by the canons, according to a custom that derived from a bequest by a nobleman of the city.

So, while our friend was eating, we looked round the cathedral. They say it is the most magnificent in the whole of
France. It is in the form of a cross, with a large choir all in
black and white marble. The statues are immeasurably
large and are all of bronze. The choir-stalls are of walnut,
with the finest figurative carvings one could ever see. The
stained-glass windows all have representations of the whole
of the Old Testament and are very well done.[b]

Then we took a turn through the town. It is beautiful,
very old and prosperous. It stands at the top of a low hill
and is surrounded by very strong and high walls, but it is

form a comprehensive statement of the Christian doctrines of the Fall and Redemption, in which the Old Testament is regarded as a prefiguration, or anticipation, of the New. The stained-glass windows were the work of a master verrier, *Arnaud de Moles, a Gascon, and are dated 1513. The three principal windows teach the same doctrines in scenes of the Creation and Fall, the Crucifixion and the Resurrection, accompanied by a wealth of supporting imagery.*

c *The walls were demolished in the nineteenth century and there is no record of the inscription. It would almost certainly have been headed: 'Augusta Auscorum'.*

not very large. Above the gate where we entered are carved these words, in old lettering and in stone which has been partly eroded by time: *Augusta Auxicon*. The rest cannot be read because the stone has been so badly damaged. Inside the gate is the seminary of the Barnabite Fathers, a large imposing place.[c]

From there we went to look for our companion. We then set off for Barran, two leagues away, and continued through a small place called L'Isle-de-Noé, and then to Montesquiou, another three leagues. Here we spent the evening among the heretics but, being tired, we did not bother to look round the town. In the morning we set off for Marciac.

It was a journey of three leagues, through hills and lowland, with fruit-trees everywhere, especially cherries. We called at the house of one of the local country people to ask if he would sell us some. He straight away climbed a tree and picked three or four pounds and gave them to us. He refused to take any money saying that, although he was poor, such a trifle counted for nothing. He had eleven children all of them small, so that they scarcely knew how to give one another a drink. He said his wife had died and he had to provide for all the children. Though they were peasants, they were good-looking youngsters and were well dressed, all in the same colour – a splendid sight!

We thanked him for the cherries and carried on to Marciac, a very prosperous place. We stayed the night there and

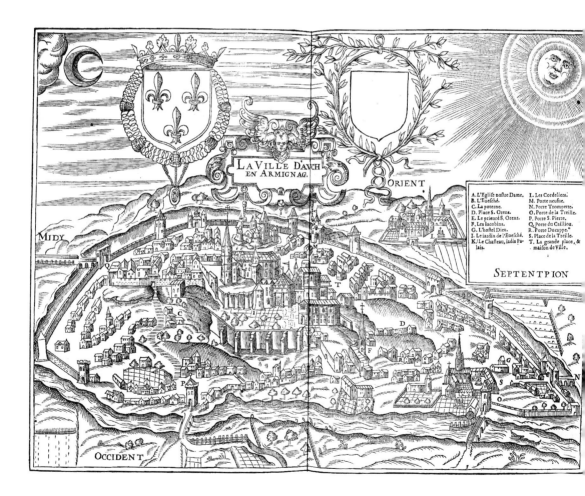

in the morning went to the monastery of the Augustinians to say Mass. We continued on to Maubourget, crossing a wide river[a] on the way. This place, two leagues on from Marciac, is true to its name,[b] having been completely shattered in the wars. There is nothing to be seen except broken walls and great heaps of stone, a sight that arouses one's pity. In spite of that the place is well-stocked and the goods are cheap. We passed through and carried on until evening when we arrived at a church where, after supper, we had to pass the night. We did not have the comfort of a bed so we slept on straw. Early next morning we set of for Anoye, two leagues away, but it was a bad road. The country was sometimes hilly, sometimes flat, but everywhere bearing fruit. We came to a river where there were many fish and razor-shells. We stopped here to wash our clothes and while they were drying in the sun we caught a lot of the shell-fish. Then, gathering up our things, we made for Anoye. It is truly a boring place, just to look at,[c] consisting of a few huts, all thatched, occupied by shepherds and the poor. We called on a woman who did us the kindness of cooking the shell-fish. She was astonished that we wanted to eat such creatures and said that they would make us ill. She had never in all her days seen anyone eat them and did not know how to cook them. We showed her how to do it.

After the meal we gave the woman a little money and set out for Morlaàs. We went through woods and chestnut groves where we found a large amount of mushrooms. While we were collecting them it began to thunder and lighten. So we gave up looking for mushrooms and ran for it. But the rain, faster than we were, caught us up from behind and chased us, willy-nilly, from under one tree to another. At the end of it we were thoroughly soaked, for it accompanied us all the way from Anoye to Morlaàs, which is two leagues.

Morlaàs is a town hidden in a hollow between hills and trees so that you can hardly see it as you approach. We entered through a gate that seemed to be the entrance to the very house of the Devil. So I believed it to be because they were all heretics here and not a Catholic among them. When we saw so much of the Devil's work, on no account would we pass through the town so we came out of the gate again. There we met a Franciscan Observantine and were greatly cheered that we had come upon the friar because it

Fig. 36 *View of the city of Auch about 1575. It had changed little by the time of Laffi's visit a century later. (From Belleforest, François de,* Cosmographie universelle, *1575.)*

B *Lescar was the Roman town of
Beneharnum, which gave its name
to the ancient province of Béarn,
and was its capital until overrun
by the Moors in 841. The bishop-
ric was suppressed in 1790 following the Revolution.*

was evening. He took us to his hut where we met his companion and stayed for the evening. They gave us bread and
wine for supper, together with a little soup, seeking our
sympathy because the heretics offered them no charity.
Many times had they been about to leave the place for good
but their provincial superior would not allow it. It was he
who provided them with bread and wine.

The fathers then questioned us about our homeland and
we told them about it and gave them some holy medals,
which they greatly appreciated. In the morning we thanked
them, took up our belongings and left the town to follow
the road to Arber,[a] about three leagues distant. But we had
hardly gone half a league before we came to a great river. So
our Roman companion had to take his shoes off and firstly
carry our packs across and then us. Once over the river we
came across a peasant and asked him the way to Arber. He
said this was not the right road and would take us much
longer. We should do better to recross the river and make
for the town of Lescar, which would make our journey
much shorter. We thanked him and returned across the
river using the same bridge provided by our companion.
We followed the road the local fellow had indicated but
walked all day without finding Lescar. Nor did we know
where we were going, walking all the while through dark
woods without meeting anyone to show us the way. Finally,
as the sun was setting, we arrived at Lescar.[b]

The town lies in a flat region and is surrounded by very
tall trees so that you do not see it until you reach the walls.
It is a fine place. The inhabitants are half Catholics, half
heretics. There is a seminary that teaches all branches of
learning. It is run by the Barnabite Fathers who give generous alms to pilgrims, as does the bishop. While our companion went to the seminary to receive charity – and also from
the bishop – we went to an inn. Here there were many students who asked us, in Latin, what town and country we
were from and we replied we were Italians and Romans.
After asking us many things they paid for our drinks. We
thanked them and as we were leaving the inn we encoun-
tered a local fellow who was drunk. He took us by the hand
and, with much ceremony, invited us to take a drink with
him, saying he wanted to pay for a jugful – which they call
a 'pot'. In return, we were to pray to God for him on our
journey.

After much trouble we rid ourselves of the drunkard and went to rejoin our companion. He was at the door of the seminary absorbing a rural 'branch of learning' in the shape of a great dish of soup and mutton that the Fathers had given him. When he had finished we set off all together on our way. After half a league we came to a village where we stayed the night at the house of a wealthy country-man. He treated us very well and would take nothing from us. Next morning we thanked him and made our way to Orthez, two leagues away, walking across a broad plain.

Orthez is a very fine village, as large as a town and sur-rounded by a very strong wall. But it is full of heretics. We went to the vicar to have the dimissory signed so that we could celebrate Mass next morning, which would be the feast of Corpus Christi. After that we went to look for lodg-ings. In the end we went to an inn that was run by a heretic, who looked after us very well. Next morning we rose and went to say Mass at the Capuchins', which was outside the town where there are only a few Catholics. Then we went to join the procession of the Host where we saw those heret-ical scoundrels. They were at the windows, with hats on their heads, laughing like lunatics while the procession passed. The vicar had issued a proclamation that they should all stay indoors lest they gave offence or hindered the ecclesiastical business, which was why they were at their windows laughing and jeering. When the procession was over, a blessing was given in the church. The church really is very badly looked after, it is more like a stall for cattle than a church or a house of God. We departed from Orthez, leaving behind our Roman companion who was sick. On leaving the town you cross a splendid bridge which has a very high tower at each end.[c]

Then you come to a small town, and after that you reach Sauveterre-de-Béarn, five leagues away. This is the first place in the province of Cantabria. It is very pleasant and livelier than Orthez, but not so big. It lies in a beautiful plain with meadows, orchards, vineyards and other de-lights. We stayed the night here and in the morning con-tinued on our way to St-Jean-Pied-de-Port. After one league we came to a village called St Palais. Beyond it are woods and coppices of chestnut. We got lost among the chestnuts, until at last we met a woman who was going to Mass and asked her, please God, to show us the right road

Fig. 37 *The gatehouse on the Vieux Pont, Orthez.*

that we had missed. She courteously led us to the road we were seeking. Here we came to a small village and, still carrying on through the chestnuts, we reached another village where a priest was sitting at the door of his church. We had a long conversation, after which he brought us fruit and something to drink and showed us the right road to take. We thanked him and carried on to St-Jean-Pied-de-Port, a distance of three leagues.

Before leaving this province I will mention in a couple of words some of the things I noticed everywhere. Firstly, since they live half among the Pyrenees, people here make candles from pine-resin instead of wax. They give a very good light and have a pleasant smell. There is also a great shortage of wine, so ordinary families who cannot buy any have to do it this way: they buy a cask of strong wine vinegar and when they want a drink they take a jug of water and add a glass of vinegar to it. They also do this whenever a stranger asks them for a drink. Everyone, except the grander gentry, wears wooden shoes and, instead of a hat, they have a beret as big as a trencher which falls on each side like an umbrella. Their cloaks are very large and instead of a collar they have a hood such as a friar wears, together with various accessories. Likewise, round the neck they wear a ruff, like the Germans. They are a very proud people, though their dress looks very outlandish and absurd.

And so we continued on our way until we reached St-Jean-Pied-de-Port. It is the last town that belongs to the king of France. It is quite big and lies at the foot of a high hill, at the top of which is a citadel with a strong garrison. So the town is well defended and well equipped to be a frontier town. Fruit and wine are very plentiful here and they begin to sell Spanish wines, which we tasted. We continued on our way for the sun was still high in the sky. We walked all the while between precipitous mountains, which are terrifying just to look at. They seemed as if they were always about to fall on top of you. Night fell while we were still among these precipices. We were getting desperate lest we fail to find a house to shelter in. We did not know what to do, no longer able to see the path, the night was so dark. At last we saw a light far off among the steep hills and made our way towards it as best we could.

When we reached it we addressed the owner of the place, who appeared at a window: 'We are poor pilgrims

Fig. 38-39 *Examples of Béarnaise dress, from a map of the Béarn, about 1650. (Archives Départementales, Pau.)*

There is an 11th-century record of a monastery called San Salvador on the pass of Ibañeta, where Laffi and his companion rested. It is described in 12th-century documents as 'Charlemagne's chapel.' It was deserted when Laffi saw it. His is the only known reference to wall paintings and sculpture.

and men of the Church who have got lost in the mountains.' We begged him, by the bowels of God's mercy, that over and above any charity he might bestow on us, we might give him whatever payment should be due to him. Although he hardly understood our language, nor we his, he immediately agreed and opened his door to us. We entered the house and he led us upstairs into a room where he had a great fire because it is always cold here amid the ice and snow. We warmed ourselves beside the fire while he laid a table with what few things he had. After supper we said the litany of the Blessed Virgin and other prayers, as was our custom. The man had many small daughters and after we had finished our prayers the smallest of them came up to kiss my hand. She then struck her hand two or three times on the palm and the back of my hand and did the same to her father and mother and also to my companion and the other members of the household. Such are the ceremonies they perform in the province of Cantabria.

Next morning, before we left, we tried to settle our account with our host, but he would take nothing, saying he was not an innkeeper and that what he had done we must accept for the love of God. We thanked him for his great kindness and continued on our way. We kept on climbing the very high and rugged hills for a stretch of seven leagues. It was a frightening and dangerous journey. In the end, with the help of God and St James of Galicia we reached the very top of the Pyrenees. This is where France and the province of Cantabria ends. There is a small, very old chapel here. We went in – there are neither doors nor windows that can be closed – and sang the 'Te Deum Laudamus', to give thanks to God for having brought us here safe and sound, in his infinite mercy.

But before leaving the summit of these very high Pyrenees, which we had climbed with such effort, we rested awhile in the chapel. In it you can see some old figurative painting and sculpture. There are also a number of inscriptions but they are too worn away, because of their age, to be legible.[a] From here you can see France to the east and Spain to the west. This is the very place where Roland sounded his horn when he called Charlemagne to his aid. He blew it so hard that it split. I have seen it with my own eyes, as I shall tell you later when I describe the defeat at Roncesvalles.

Fig. 40 *The chapel at Ibañeta. It was severely damaged during the French Revolution but restorations were undertaken by the Colegiata of Roncesvalles in 1849. It was used as a refuge for travellers until destroyed by fire in 1884. This drawing was done between 1875 and 1884.* (From Veillet, Chanon René, Recherches sur la ville et sur l'église de Bayonne, *1929; vol. 3.)*

While we were resting I told my companion about the first time I went to St James of Galicia in 1666 with three companions, though we had then taken a different road.

8

THE 'SAINT OF ASPET'

Another way from Toulouse

A *The regular pilgrimage roads between France and Spain were over the Pyrenees, either by way of the pass of Roncevalles in the west, or over the much lower pass at the eastern end of the range, south of Perpignan. Laffi twice took another, more adventurous route across the central Pyrenees. This took him from St-Gaudens over the pass of Bielsa (now a tunnel), and then to Barbastro.*

I MADE THE JOURNEY FROM TOULOUSE TO Madrid twice, in 1666 and 1673. This was the first and the third time I visited these parts. On leaving Toulouse we crossed the bridge I have already described and headed south through Gascony. Our intention was to go to Madrid and thence to Galicia. For the reader's pleasure and, even more, for the sake of the next people who want to make the same journey from Toulouse to Madrid, a road which has never been undertaken by the stage coach nor even by any wayfarer, I shall set it down here, together with the number of leagues from one place to the next.[a]

We turned south, as I said, passing through countryside that was always lovely, with thriving fields, vineyards, market-gardens and splendid mansions. We came to a town called Villeneuve, one league from Toulouse and, after another league, to Seysses, and then Ox, another league. They are all delightful, charming places, belonging to the Count of Toulouse. From here we went to Cazères, a distance of three leagues; then to a place called Martres-Tolosane, one more league, and then to St-Martory, another league. We were still crossing flat countryside that has no equal as regards the qualities I have mentioned. After St-Martory we went to St-Gaudens, another three leagues.

St-Gaudens is a very big town and stands at the top of a pleasant hill, not far from the river that passes through Toulouse. It is a market town, well fortified and surrounded by good walls and a moat. There are religious houses of nuns and monks. We stayed here for the feast of Pentecost. About three leagues to the south, among the foothills is Mont Aspet, a place we were taken to see by our host where we were lodging. It is a little village, half way up the hill, and consists of a few small houses and huts. In one of them was a man, half wasted away, who lay stretched out on a big wooden table. He was covered with a white sheet and a blanket as though he were on a sick-bed. His features were emaciated, giving him a cadaverous appearance. The people who were looking after him uncovered him so that we could see the rest of his body, with its belly, back, arms and legs all wasted away. His finger-nails and toe-nails were so long they curled round many times, not like yours or mine.

I tell you, this man had no flesh on him, except some on his face. He was, as I said, very wasted. He kept his mouth tight shut and his teeth clenched, and only moved his lips when he spoke. The people who were watching over him would feed him with broth, in drops at a time, putting it into his mouth through a gap where a tooth was missing, by means of a little drinking cup. Anyone who had not seen him would not believe it. But I saw him with my own eyes and, even so, I felt I could not believe it. But I have for witnesses three companions who actually saw him with me. They were Sig. D. Morando Conti, Sig. Nicolò Mantuani, and Sig. Francesco Magnani, all three from Bologna. We stood there talking with him for three or four hours. He discourses very well in all languages, and he told us a few things about his life.

First, he was a doctor and had studied at the University of Paris. He had been in the present condition for fourteen years and ate nothing else but what we had seen. He also told us that his name was Jean Rofat and that he took this self-chastisement upon himself as a penance for his sins. He desired that all men in the world, both good and evil, should come to see him, so that the good might persevere in doing good and the evil learn to fear God, turn from the path of wrong-doing and serve the supreme Creator of all things. He also said that, in spite of his condition, he fasted every Friday in honour of Christ's passion.

Meanwhile, others arrived who had come from afar, so we gave way to them. But before we left he made us write our names, surnames, nationality and where we were going in a great book. He made all strangers from distant parts do the same. Then, bidding us a last farewell, he told us to be joyful and to pray to God for him, saying these very words:

Andate pur andate, non saran sparsi i vostri passi in vano. [Go then, go; your steps will not have been taken in vain.]

A *Laffi's description of the man once known as the 'saint of Aspet' is confirmed in a report by a government official, Louis de Froideur, who was visiting the region in 1667 (Ousset, P.-E., 'Les registres paroissiaux d'Aspet antérieurs à la Révolution': extrait de la* Revue de Comminges, *1946-7, Toulouse, 1947). He was astonished by the man's serenity in view of his appalling and unremitting physical suffering, which was brought on by a general paralysis. His death certificate, drawn up by the parish priest, who was a relation, gives his name as Jean Ruffart and the date of death as 28 November 1672. He was born about 1640. Laffi is often inaccurate about details of this kind. The meeting took place in 1666. Laffi passed through St-Gaudens again in 1673 hoping for another meeting with Ruffart, only to learn that he had died the previous year. He heard much more from the Dominican Fathers of St-Gaudens with whom he lodged on his second visit. Ruffart earned a reputation locally as a miracle-worker and prophet.*

So people came to this place from all parts, from nearby as well as from afar, to seek his advice in their troubles. After seeing him and hearing his words they were comforted and greatly reassured. The innkeeper who took us to him told us that, on occasions, he foretold the future. We returned to St-Gaudens.[a]

In 1673 when, as I told you, I went to Galicia for the third time, being in Toulouse, I was very curious to see this man once more, if he were still alive. I was in the company of Fra Giuseppe Liparini, whom I have already mentioned. We passed through the same villages and reached St-Gaudens where we took a meal at the monastery of the Dominican fathers. They looked after us very well, treating us with great kindness and generosity, for Liparini had a letter of recommendation from his Vicar-General, Father Passarini. After the meal we thanked the fathers and told them we wished to go up to Aspet to see the 'skin-and-bone-man', whose name was Jean Rofat. But they said he was no longer there, for he had died. We were very disappointed to hear this, not so much on my account, but for my companion who had been very anxious to see this prodigy – and because we had made such a long detour off the regular route. However, we were reconciled when the fathers recounted part of the man's life story to us. To give you a taste of it, dear reader, I shall relate two or three episodes, which occurred not long before he died.

The fathers told us that this man had been regarded as a saint by the people and that he died on the 20 August, 1672. He was buried in the village of Aspet itself. This lay in the barony of an heretical prince who was also lord of many other places in the region. Jean Rofat was stricken with his cruel infirmity at the age of nineteen when he was in the finest flower of his youth. The disease remained with him until the end of his painful and bitter life at the age of thirty-seven. This man, who had passed such a wretched and cruel life for a span of eighteen years – from nineteen to thirty-seven, to be precise – then departed this vale of tears.

Among the many things the fathers told us I will relate only two so as not to bore the reader. One day, while Rofat was counselling and instructing the people, telling them in particular about the dreadful last day of Universal Judgement, he suddenly stopped speaking and remained still for

This episode must refer to the great earthquake in 1660 that began at night and was said to have been felt across the whole of France. It was most severe in the central Pyrenees. Ruffart must have detected the first tremors. According to de Froideur, 'Everyone, in order to save themselves, ran out as fast as they could in their nightwear, for fear of being crushed under the ruins. It was a dreadful thing to see all the naked people shouting and weeping in the middle of the streets, searching fruitlessly for shelter in the ruins of the crumbling houses' (Ousset, op. cit.).

the space of about a quarter of an hour, seemingly without drawing breath. It was as if he were meditating on some great thing. Suddenly his tongue was unloosed and, with a dreadful shout, he cried, 'Quickly! Get out! The house is going to fall down!' The people round him, all of them still in a state of awe from his preaching, stood as if completely bereft of their senses, not knowing which way to flee, and staring at one another unable to utter even a word. Again he shouted, this time louder, that they must fly from the danger that threatened. Then they took flight, some by the stairs and some by the windows. In an instant the house, that a moment ago had been full, was now empty. Those who were minding Rofat took hold of the table on which he lay, ran downstairs and carried him outside. They had hardly gone more than one step out of the door when the house collapsed to its very foundations, in full view of the people who had just left, and also the rest of the village.[a]

When the news reached the heretical prince who was lord and master of the village, that Jean Rofat's house had collapsed and how everything had turned out, he was greatly astonished. At the same time, having been brought up in no other school except the teachings of Calvin, it was much to his taste that this had happened to a Catholic, and in particular to this poor young man who, because of his cruel and peculiar infirmity, was well-known throughout the whole region and beyond. Smiling with no little satisfaction he told his wife, the princess, and she, being curious, as is the way with ladies, told her husband she wanted to go and see for herself. It was not far away, only two leagues.

The lady left the castle on a litter, with her many servants, eager to discover the truth about the matters that had been told her. She soon reached the village she sought, with her retinue, and alighted from the litter. She observed the wretched house, buried in its own ruins, and asked where was the young man whom she wished to see. She was taken to the place where he lay. He was on the table that for so many years had served him as a feather-bed and that would eventually serve him as a boat in which to depart from the tempestuous ocean which is this world.

When she caught sight of the dreadful spectacle, the like of which she had never set eyes on before, she was held in suspense for a long time before she could finally bring herself to speak. Thereafter she conversed with him at length on various subjects. Having thus satisfied herself about everything, she made a sign to her servants that she wished to leave. To the young man she said that he must bear his wretched condition and grave illness with patience, for God would recompense him in heaven. Whether she spoke sincerely or with the intention of mocking the Catholic faith I do not know for only God understands the motives of such people. To this the young man replied that but for our hope of reward in heaven by God, the Creator of all things, and our dying in his grace, we who are Catholics would be lost and without hope in the midst of the persecutions and travails of this life. She answered, 'We, too, hope for the same thing,' to which he rejoined, 'Yes, but only so long as you die in the Catholic faith.' But she replied, 'It matters not, either you in mine or I in yours.' After more argument – and, God knows, it was giving her no joy to speak in this manner – she finally said she wished to die in that faith in which God had placed her in the beginning.

After a short silence the young man spoke. 'You, my lady, will die under Catholic law and the Roman apostolic tradition. As a sign of this, I tell you – and it will come true – at the end of two months the prince, your husband, will die. You will then forswear your heresy at the hands of a Dominican father and embrace the Catholic faith.' Hearing these words she replied with a smile, 'All things are possible, but I find that very hard to believe.' With that she departed, and returned to the castle to tell her husband everything. After she left the young man uttered not another word to those standing around him, for the space of about an hour. They had noted carefully all that had passed between him and the lady. They well knew that very often what he foretold did indeed come to pass, so they related everything to the Dominican fathers of St-Gaudens. The latter replied that it would give them great joy if things turned out as Rofat had prophesied, and many of them remained confident about it.

A few days later the young man, being wholly resigned to the will of God, and after discoursing on divine things to the people round to hear him, rendered up his spirit to the Lord. That was on August 20, 1672, as I said earlier. In their minds he ranked among the saints, so they buried him in a place apart, and hoped he would give them some sign,

*There seems to be no record in any
local archives to support any part
of this story. From 1608 Aspet
came directly under the jurisdic-
tion of the Crown, and both lords
and commoners seem to have been
solidly Catholic. The 'Protestant
prince' and his wife, if they existed
at all, can have been only fleeting
birds of passage. The reputation
of the 'saint of Aspet', never very
widely known, did not long sur-
vive his death. He was buried in
Aspet church. The present writer
has searched for his tomb, so far
without success.*

which he did. Thus, on the sixtieth day, that is to say, at the
end of two months when he predicted to the lady that her
husband would die, the latter was sitting at table with some
of his kinsmen, whom he had invited to a meal. Whether it
was by chance or whether God disposed it thus, they found
themselves witnesses to what happened next. After general
conversation, as is usual among guests round a table, the
lady recalled – it may even have been by God's intention –
what had passed between her and the young man at Aspet.
'O my lord,' she said laughingly to her husband, 'do you not
also remember the exact prophecy that young man of Aspet
made to me, how you would die? It seems to me that his
prophecy has now been proved false, because here you are
among your relations and friends. You have triumphed
and many scorn whomsoever of the Catholics you meet.'
Everyone laughed, including the lady, and when they had
stopped she told them everything that had passed between
her and the young man who had died.

Their conversation over, they rose from the table, still
laughing and making jokes about Catholics. The prince
took two steps and, without uttering a word, not even 'O
God', fell dead. The guests were all terrified, their laughter
turning to tears at such a tragic turn of events. After the
burial, which was performed according to their rites, they
all went home talking about it, as people do, for seven or
eight days.

As for the lady, when she saw that what the young man
had foretold had indeed come about, she lost no time in ne-
gotiating her own salvation. She sent for the Dominican
fathers of St-Gaudens and told them everything that had
happened. A few days later, after receiving instruction
from the Father Prior and in the presence of many other
fathers and priors, she renounced heresy. Today she leads
an exemplary life. She does much for charity, restoring
churches and performing other pious works as a true child
of the Catholic faith, so may it bring happiness in this life
and glory in the next. That is as much, dear reader, that
I can tell you about the life of Jean Rofat, as it was told to
me by the Dominican fathers of St-Gaudens. Except that,
in 1666, as I told you, I saw him with my own eyes and
heard him speak.[a]

After leaving St-Gaudens we came to a town called Mont-
réjeau, a distance of two leagues, and then La-Barthe-de-

B *Not identified – perhaps Ara-gnouet.*

C *Now a road tunnel.*

D *The Cinca.*

E *The town is still girded by a wall. It overlooks the confluence of the Cinca and the Ara rivers.*

F *Naval.*

G *They are still working salt-pans along the upper course of the River Cinca. Below Bielsa is the river-side town of Salinas (= salt-pan) de Bielsa.*

Neste, another two. Here you begin to enter the high Pyrenees and come to a place called Sarrancolin, a large, walled town, exactly two leagues further. From here we went to Arreau, another large town one league on, which was beside a river between very high mountains. From Arreau you go two leagues to Ospitale, the last town in France.[b] You then climb to the pass of Bielsa,[c] under the high peaks of the Pyrenees and thereafter, descending continually, you reach the town of the same name, Bielsa, which is another four leagues. This is the first town in Spain and the kingdom of Aragon. From here you follow a river[d] until you reach the village of Labuerda, four leagues, and then a fortified town called Ainsa, two leagues. It has a fine, strong castle and a well-armed garrison, being near the frontier. The castle stands on a promontory overlooking the mouth of the river that comes down from the Pyrenees.[e]

Four leagues from here is another, bigger fortified town[f] in more fertile land. They do much trade because of a salt-water river which runs here. On its banks they manufacture quantities of salt. They make large amounts of a white salt that has no equal, and send it not only throughout Spain but also through the whole of France.[g]

From Naval we went three leagues to Barbastro, a fine city, its lands abundant in every kind of fruit, which is forever in season, for it seems to always spring in this place.

From here we went to Peralta de Alcofea, two leagues, then Poleñino, four leagues, and Alcubierre, two leagues. Along this way you go through somewhat hilly country, thickly wooded, where all kinds of animals are hunted. Another two leagues and you come to Leciñena, and then Perdiguera, one league. They lie in a plain where there are many fields and vines. Another three leagues on is Villamayor, truly a splendid place. It is large, pleasant and has everything in plenty. It is rightly called *villa mayor*, the chief town, because it is situated in such a beautiful agreeable setting, with gardens, palaces, orchards and vineyards – one can say no more. It is only one league from here to Zaragoza, through similar countryside. From Zaragoza we went to Madrid and thence to Compostella. But, for now, I shall not describe the journey there, which I did in stages. I shall leave that for the return journey, as I shall be following the same route.

Finisterre

Padrón

SANTIAGO DE
COMPOSTELA

R Miño

Portomarin

Cebrero

Ponferrada

Astorga

LEÓN

Sahagún

Fromista

BURGOS

Silos

SANTO DOMINGO
DE LA CALZADA

LOGROÑO

Estella

PAMPLONA

Roncesvalles

R Ebro

Bay of
Biscay

FRANCE

SPAIN

0   Kilometres   100

RONCESVALLES TO PAMPLONA

9

THE PALADINS

Roncesvalles to Pamplona

A *Laffi is referring to the* Capilla de Sancti Spiritus, *the chapel of the Holy Spirit, which once held some thirty tombs. The building was originally a funerary chapel and ossuary for pilgrims who died in the hospital. Many bones still lie in an underground chamber below the altar. Later, it was claimed that the chapel was built over the rock that Roland, the hero of Ronces-valles, split with his sword when he was near death; and that the bones were those of the knights who died with him on the battle-field. The tombs were all destroyed early in the 19th century.*

B *In fact, usually to the left.*

———

Fig. 41 *An architect's impression of the chapel of the Holy Spirit, Roncesvalles, about the time of its construc-tion (12th century?), and before the addition of the cloister. (From Veillet, op. cit., Fig. 40.)*

———

O N L E A V I N G T H E C H A P E L W E W E N T D O W N for about a quarter of a league until we came to Roncesvalles, the place we so much longed to reach. It is hidden by the slope and by dense trees, so you come upon it quite unexpectedly and all the more gladly. While we were thinking we still had far to go, we found ourselves at its very door. We went down a paved walk and under a great arch. On the right are many ancient tombs contain-ing the remains of kings, dukes, marquises, counts, pal-adins and lords who died in that great feat of arms that is renowned down the centuries.[a]

The main church lies to the left. It is very old indeed. It was built by Charlemagne and Bishop Turpin said Mass there. When we arrived they were singing the solemn Mass, with music, in the Spanish style. The only instru-ments they had were bagpipes of various kinds. They made a deafening noise that could easily be heard a mile away. The organ pipes are made of tin and wood and when it is played they, too, sound like bagpipes with drones. For all we could tell, their sounds were indistinguishable from one another and were very monotonous to the ear, being all much the same tone.

There are many canons who are dressed in this fashion: they wear a long black cassock, like other Spanish priests. On the cassock is a green cross, on the breast, over the heart. The upper part of the cross curves round to the right[b] like a bishop's crosier. When they go into the choir they wear a small white rochet and a mozzetta that has the same cross on it. They perform the offices very well with due solemnity and much reverence. They keep their church bright and polished, like all the other churches in Spain. We entered the sacristy to ask if we might celebrate Mass.

A This was not the only church claiming to possess Roland's horn. As the legends of the heroes of Roncesvalles became more and more widely disseminated their relics multiplied in other churches along the pilgrimage roads, especially in France. From the end of the 11th century another horn, also said to be Roland's, was displayed in the church of St-Seurin at Bordeaux. His tomb, together with those of other knights, could be seen at Arles in the Alyscamps and at Blaye in the church of

Having done so, we thanked the sacristan, and received absolution at the high altar. It is a very fine, ancient altar with a solemn image of the Blessed Virgin, and has a great many big, silver lamps.

In front of the altar is a high iron grille that has Roland's horn fixed to the top. It is about two *braccia* long and is made all in one piece. It has a split down one side from which the air escapes when it is blown. They say it was caused by Roland at that moment, on the heights of the Pyrenees, when he blew it to call Charlemagne. The king was waiting at St-Jean-Pied-de-Port for Roland, who had gone to Marsilion, the king of Aragon, to collect tribute.[a]

Beside the horn are two iron maces. One was Roland's,

St-Romain, *as well as at Ronces-*
valles. See further: Lejeune, Rita,
and Stiennon, Jacques, La lé-
gende de Roland dans l'art du
moyen âge (2 vols), pp. 365-6,
Brussels, 1966.

B *Renaud.*

C *A 'span'.*

D *The plate, called a* pax brede *or*
osculatorium, was made of ivory,
wood or metal. It had a handle on
the back and bore a representation
of a religious subject, usually the
Crucifixion. It came into use in
the later Middle Ages, but is now
obsolete in the West.

the other Rinaldo's[b] which they used in battle and kept attached to the saddle-bow. This is the way they are made: they used a very thick baton of wood, about the length of one's arm, at one end of which is an iron chain, about a palm[c] in length. At the other end of the chain is a big iron ball, eight-sided or some other shape. You can also see Roland's iron stirrups and his ankle-boots which, they say, he would change into for Mass, which he sang with much solemnity.

We left the church and went through the town to see what still remained from the old days. Outside, only a few steps away to the west, is a little chapel that Charlemagne had built after Roland and the other paladins died. We went in and found they were saying Mass, so we waited until it was finished. Their Mass is different from ours in certain respects. Just before the Elevation they consecrate the bread and cut it into little pieces. Then at the communion, they dispense it by carrying it through the church in a bowl covered with a white napkin. Also, they kiss a large metal plate, where we would give one another the Kiss of Peace. In this chapel no one may say Mass who is not ordained.[d]

The chapel is square but not very high. It is situated, so they say, on the exact spot where Roland stood after the second battle, weeping for his men. He uttered some such words as these: 'O grievous, O unhappy valley, now you will be for ever bloody!' They also say that all the barons who were present begged Roland to sound his horn. But he answered them saying, however much they urged him to sound it, he would not do so from fear, nor to bring Charlemagne to his aid. He would never sound it out of cowardice.

Seeing that the field had already been lost in the first and second battles and that the valley was full of dead, he sighed and groaned. He wanted to exhort his men, but his grief prevented him from speaking. For it was he who had led his people into the massacre at Roncesvalles. At length he recovered his voice as best he could, and once more spurred them on, in a long and learned speech, to fight yet again for the holy faith. When he had finished everyone leapt to their horses and, commending themselves to God and his most holy Mother, began the third and final battle. It was very bloody and terrible and lasted all day which, some say, was the feast of St Michael. Of all the enemy army

Fig. 42 An architect's
impression of the chapel of
the Holy Spirit with its cloister,
first mentioned in 1624 (Jean de
Huarte, Histoire manuscrite
de Roncevaux*). Huarte also*
refers to wall-paintings, tombs
and tombstones within the
cloister. (From Veillet,
op. cit., Fig. 40.)

comprising, besides many kings, dukes and lords, some six hundred thousand men, there remained alive only two, namely King Marsilion and Baligant. Of the Christian army, of whom there were about twenty thousand and six hundred, there remained only three: Rinaldo, Ricciardetto[a] and Turpin.

Roland, seeing all his people lost, withdrew to his tent. Now, having decided to sound his horn, he climbed to the top of the hill so that Charlemagne should hear him. Then he blew with all his might and Charlemagne did hear. To some people this appears to have been a miracle, but it is credible because, from the place where he sounded it to St-Jean-Pied-de-Port is only six and a half leagues. They say that he blew so hard that, the third time, blood spurted from his mouth and nose. As for the horn, it split down one side, as I have seen it cleft with my own eyes. After sounding it he returned to his tent, glancing round at the now

Fig. 43 *The chapel of the Holy Spirit today, much restored.*

Fig. 44 *The distinctive emblem of the religious community of Roncesvalles, a cross and crosier combined.*

ravaged field but seeing none of the enemy with whom he might give battle. Tired out from the long fighting and from sounding his horn, that had made so much blood issue from his mouth and nose, he could no longer stay on his horse. He approached the foot of the hill where there is a spring – known to this day as Roland's spring[b] – dismounted and drank two or three draughts. At that very moment his horse fell dead, covered with wounds from the fighting. The say he wept, having been served so bravely by it.

Then he looked all about him, in case he might see his cousin Rinaldo in that valley full of dead. He shuddered to see so many and wept for his own men, calling them blessed, because they had fought so nobly for the holy faith and for their country. And he was ever bemoaning the treachery of Ganelon and King Marsilion. He looked around yet again, in case he should see someone, but could not discern a single soul still living. So, calling upon death, he grasped his sword, Durendal, for the last time and struck it against a rock. But however often he did so he was unable to break it. Indeed, he finally gave it such a blow that it split the rock. But by now the sword had cracked, near the hilt. I myself have seen it, in the gallery of the king of Spain.

Then Roland turned to his sword and said, 'O strong Durendal, had I known thee at first as I know thee now at my death, I should have held the world of little account. Nor should I have come to this pass. I have spared thee many times in war, not knowing how much virtue resided in thee.' As he spoke thus he saw Rinaldo come. Though he had already fallen from weakness, he rose and took four steps to meet his cousin but, unable to stand, he fell once more. Rinaldo came to him and comforted him, followed by Turpin, Ricciardetto and another man of religion. Roland told them he was now summoned by death and that no more time remained to him in this life.

Then he knelt as best as he could to make confession. He wept bitterly for the sins he confessed, begging the Lord's forgiveness. Then he took off his armour, saying, 'Lord, behold your armour and behold your soldier, turned grey-haired in the wars fought in defence of your faith. Now it is time I should rest in the peace of your glory.' Then he made a long and ardent prayer, to which heaven answered that, if he still wished to remain among the living, God would grant him such men and weapons as would make the whole

A *Laffi gives as the principal source of his account the* Rotta di Roncisvalle, dove morì Orlando con tutti i Paladini. *It was printed in Florence in the early 16th century. He accordingly uses the Italian forms of proper names.*

B *Again, this must be the chapel of the Holy Spirit where Laffi saw the tombs. It is exactly square and is known to have contained wall paintings (no longer extant) depicting the battle. The accompanying inscriptions are known to have included the names of Roland, Oliver, Guy de Bourgogne, Thierry d'Ardennes and Riol du Mas, among others. It is inferred from this that the source of the paintings was a* chanson de geste *'Fierbras' (c. 1170) in which the same names occur.*

The defeat of the Christian army on the Pass of Roncesvalles took place in 778 when the rearguard of Charlemagne's forces, returning from a campaign against the Moors in Spain, was ambushed by a body of Basques who committed wholesale slaughter and pillage. A biographer of Charlemagne records that among the dead was 'Roland, lord of the Breton Marches' (Einhard, The Life of Charlemagne *in* Two lives of Charlemagne, *transl. L. Thorpe, Harmondsworth, 1969, pp. 64-5). The disaster inspired a great series of epic poems, written mainly in France between the eleventh and thirteenth centuries, the earliest of which was the* Chanson de Roland *(late eleventh century). They provided source-material for Italian, German and other writers, as well as a great fund of heroic themes for painters and sculptors. The meagre*

world tremble. But he replied that he desired death. Then, bending his head low, all the while asking God's forgiveness and calling on death, he commended all Christians to the eternal Father. Then, raising himself to his feet and weeping loudly, he embraced Rinaldo and the others and, lifting his eyes to heaven, said, 'Lord, I commend my soul into thy hands. You know, O Lord, that I have always yearned to die for your holy faith.'

He took two or three steps, fell to his knees once more and then to the ground. He lay there facing heavenwards, his arms stretched out like a cross, and gave up his spirit.[a] On the very spot where Roland confessed, only two or three paces from the little chapel, Charlemagne had a tomb built and buried him. The tomb is made like this: it consists of a chapel, exactly square, each side being twenty feet long. It has a pyramid-shaped dome with a cross on top. Inside is the tomb itself, also square. Between the walls and the tomb there is room for only one person. They say there may be other knights buried with Roland. On the four walls are depicted all the battles which took place here, and also the betrayal. It is painted in contrasting colours. Just beside the doorway of the tomb is the rock that Roland split. It is near the spring, as I mentioned, and is cut in two, as all may see.[b]

We never tired of admiring all this and would have stayed longer, but we were determined to visit the village. It is a very pleasant place because it is very old and lies between high mountains on a flat open space that is about half a mile round. It is surrounded not only by mountains, but by big, thickly growing trees. It was on this little, level space that the great battle took place. Later, they had it surrounded by a high, very strong fence, so that no animals of any sort could get in. It is held in deep reverence, as if it were an actual cemetery. The houses are unremarkable, though strongly built. There is a big, excellent hospice where pilgrims can stay and have three days board and lodging. They are well looked after. It is one of the wealthiest hospices to be found anywhere along the pilgrimage roads.[c]

In the evening, after supper, we went to the square to get a little fresh air and found people playing a kind of ball game. This is the way they played it: there are four wooden posts placed at the corners of the ground to form an exact

historical data was embellished with a wealth of legend that often bore no relation to the facts. The Basque enemy at Roncesvalles, for example, was appropriately transformed into Saracens.

c *The Royal Hospice was founded in 1132 by Sancho de Larrosa, bishop of Pamplona. An early thirteenth-century document in the hospital's archives describes the services offered to pilgrims: hot water to wash their clothes; baths; razors for shaving; barbers to cut their hair and cobblers to mend their shoes. They fed 'up to thirty-thousand pilgrims a year' not counting the poor and beggars, though such figures should not be taken literally. These services were still being supplied in the eighteenth century.*

square. Each player has a wooden ball, the same size as the ball we use for bowls. He also has a bat, which has a handle and a hollowed-out groove down the middle, like a piece of gutter. Then they have an iron ring in the middle of the field of play. They shoot the ball, using the bat in such a way that it runs along the groove. Their aim is to get it inside the ring. A player who fails to do so loses his ball to his opponent. If it goes outside the field of play, that is to say, beyond the four posts, he also loses. They always strike with the bat. There are always two players and whoever wins twelve balls has won the game. We stayed there until they had finished and then returned promptly to the hospice. For we meant to leave early next morning, having already been there for two days.

So, next morning we left Roncesvalles. Before departing, however, we wanted to see Roland's tomb once more. We told ourselves, only God can say whether we shall have another opportunity. We gazed at it for a long time and then scratched our names and surnames with the point of a knife on one of the stones of the sepulchre. Then we gave a last look at Roncesvalles. It is really rich and abundant in everything, particularly livestock. After our last look at the tomb and the village, we continued on our way.

The next place is called Burguete, one league further on. In the fields we saw many shepherds and large numbers of cattle, horses, sheep, pigs and other animals. They are certainly great herdsmen. The pasture is rich and fertile. From here we made our way to the Bridge of Paradise. It is three leagues on, through woodland and forest. The going was rough and difficult, because we were unable to discover either a road or even a footpath. But then we reached the top of a hill and saw the bridge below us. We began to run down at full speed, taking huge steps, even though it was very steep and rocky. It was rather frightening because, as I said, there was no footpath nor any access to a proper road. At last, after surviving many difficulties and often in danger of falling over, we arrived at the Bridge of Paradise. Though I think of it as the Bridge of Hell.

It spans a big, deep river that runs between two high hills. It is shaded by dense trees so that the water, though it is clear, in fact looks black. It is so fast-flowing that it fills the traveller with fear and trembling. The bridge is guarded by soldiers, better described as thieves and murderers. As

A *The bridge known to pilgrims as the Bridge of Paradise spans the river Arga at the entrance to the village of Zubiri ('Bridgetown' in Basque). It was also known locally as el Puente de la Rabia from the belief that an animal could be cured of rabies by passing under it three times. Laffi's memory seems, once again, to have played him false. His description of the surroundings could be applied more fittingly to the bridge over the River Erro near Mezkiritz, a few kilometres higher up.*

B *Don Jaime (or James), lord of Torre Baja.*

it is a deserted spot they will strip passers-by of their belongings. Persons of high rank are made to pay, that is, made to give them a 'tip'. Anyone who refuses gets brutally treated. They will break open your head with their sticks and will sometimes get rid of people by making the river their grave.[a]

These so-called soldiers are in fact hired ruffians of a certain Don Caime, Lord of Torbaca[b] and a knight of the brotherhood of Córdoba. He became a bandit chief and now ravages the whole of this kingdom. He has a thousand men and assassinates whomsoever he encounters, including whole villages, which he treats very badly. This Don Caime is a knight of Córdoba and the reason he took up such an unworthy career was this. He had a brother called Manuel, who was out hunting one day with one of his dogs. As he was passing through the lands of the lords of Mendoza

(which are in the same district as this), the dog took a hare. This was observed by a peasant, who notified his masters, the Mendoza. The peasant was ordered, should the hunter return, that he was to kill the dog. Eleven days went by before Don Manuel passed through the district again. When he did, there being many hares, the dog again took one. Whereupon, the good villein, doing his master's bidding, made for the spot, fired his arquebus, and stretched the dog out on the ground. But the dog's death was swiftly avenged with the death of the 'canicidal' peasant. That done, Don Manuel hastened to tell his brother, and so, taking men, horses and money, he left the city at once. But no sooner did the news of the villein's death and the departure of Don Manuel reach the ears of the lords of Mendoza than they were on horseback and quickly followed in his tracks. When they caught up with him they slew him and all his men. So merciless were they no one was left alive in the slaughter, not even a horse.

When Don Caime heard of his brother's death he quickly gathered together a band of men, armed them well, and set off in pursuit of the Mendoza, who by now had withdrawn into a castle. But Don Caime overcame every obstacle and in no time massacred them all cruelly, not even sparing their beasts. But there was an even worse testimony to his cruelty. There was living in Córdoba, in a nunnery, only one lady of the house of Mendoza. He forced his way into the place, slew her, and thus completely wiped out the family. Having achieved that, in order to escape the hand of justice, he withdrew into the wilds with a thousand men and horses. He began to lead the kind of life I mentioned above. He kept guard on the bridge because it was wooded country through which travellers coming to Spain from France by way of Roncesvalles must pass. It was a place made strong by nature with great forests and rugged mountains surrounding it.

Don Caime plundered the district for more than forty years, doing the most atrocious things. But in the year 1672, so I heard by letter, the king sent an envoy to him to know if he was willing to go to the war in Flanders. If so, he would be pardoned (and also, thereby, be removed from the kingdom). He replied that he would not serve his majesty in such distant parts, but would gladly attend upon him in Madrid. On learning this the king, with the authority of his

Fig. 45 *The fight between Roland and the giant Ferragut of Nájera. A legendary combat that became a popular symbol of the struggle between Christians and Moors, related at length in Pseudo-Turpin's* History *(p. 120) (A capital on the Palace of the Kings of Navarre, Estella. Between 1150 and 1165.)*

colourful Spanish nobleman, be-
came an outlaw after he was found
guilty in 1648 of assassinating a
corrupt priest and also of har-
bouring a group of Valencian ban-
dits. When the justices had his
house razed to the ground he took
to the highlands around Teruel
and from that time continually
raided and plundered the towns
and villages of Aragón and Valen-
cia. Like others of his profession
in those days he was sometimes
tolerated by the authorities,
even to the extent of becoming
involved in the rivalries and in-
trigues of the Spanish Court.
I have not been able to verify
Laffi's version of events.

B *A Tuscan and papal silver coin.*

C *Perhaps Larrasoaña.*

whole council, sent his envoy once more to say that, should
he come, he would be welcomed. So he went, entering
Madrid with much pomp and a great retinue. But the next
night, which was 10 February 1672, he and all his men were
arrested. He was beheaded and his men were sent to the
galleys. He died at the age of seventy-two and the tally of
his murders was one hundred and thirty. He had a nephew
who was likewise beheaded in Madrid in 1671.[a] At the
bridge we asked which was the road to Pamplona and how
much one paid to cross over. They told us about the road
and said we should pay one silver *real* each, which is about
a *paolo*[b] in our currency. They asked us what country we
came from and where we were going. We said we were
Italians and going to Galicia. Then they let us pass, asking
us whether we should be coming this way on our return. We
said yes, so that they would let us go more readily without
harming us. We paid them plenty of compliments and courtesies, all the while in fear and trembling, because all pilgrims whom we met had been maltreated by them. At last,
with God's help, we were across, but even then, they kept
peering after us and muttering among themselves.

At last we reached a spot where they could no longer see
us. Then we took to our heels, afraid they might yet fetch us
back. We did not stop running until we reached a village
called Risogna,[c] a league away. Having arrived there, we
seemed to have entered Paradise and we thanked God and
St James for delivering us from the hands of those ruffians.
But perhaps they only let us go in order to fleece us on our
return. (We took another road back.) So, having reached
Risogna, we rested for a while. It is a very pleasant, prosperous and well-populated place like many other villages in
this neighbourhood. This was very good to see.

Not far from here, on the right, we saw a splendid, well-
fortified castle. Wanting to know what the place was, we
asked a peasant whether he could satisfy our curiosity. He
replied courteously that it was called Xaverio and was
where St Francis Xavier was born. We asked him whether
there were any relics of the saint. He said no, though there
was certainly a crucifix which, when the saint was alive,
used to sweat whenever some great event took place in
the world. After his death it began to sweat every Friday
throughout the year. In order that we might witness this
miracle, and since the place was not too far away, we said we

Laffi was misinformed or, once again, has slipped up. St Francis Xavier (1506-52), the son of a noble Spanish-Basque family, was born at Javier castle, a few miles from Sangüesa. Maybe Laffi was remembering a different journey by way of the Somport Pass. Sacred images said to behave as though they are alive are not particularly rare. Not only do they sweat but they may nod the head, shed tears or even blood. We shall meet others along the road.

wanted to go there. But, he added, this image no longer produced that effect.[d]

So we went on until we came to a great plain, where the city of Pamplona was revealed to us. We had a fine view of it in the distance because it stands on quite a high hill. It is not more than four leagues from the point at which you reach the plain.

E prenuer chappitre du quart liure
du grant Roy charlemai̇e parle de
lauision et du ſinge que charlemai̇

10

THE 'CAMINO FRANCÉS' & A SURPRISING DISH

Pamplona to Burgos

A *Laffi entered by the Portal de Francia, the 'French Gate', built in the sixteenth century. The greater part of it is still standing, together with ramparts to the north and east that overlook the River Arga. The chains which raised and lowered the drawbridge over the moat have also been preserved. A little further up is the Zumalacárregui gate. The gates are built of regular masonry. Laffi's term 'living rock'* (pietra viva) *is perhaps simply meant to distinguish it from other building materials such as brick.*

Fig. 46 *St James appearing to Charlemagne. He has pilgrim's staff, wallet and hat. The Milky Way is overhead. (From the* Grandes chroniques de Saint-Denis, c. *1420. Bibliothèque Municipale, Toulouse.)*

WHEN YOU COME TO PAMPLONA, IN ORDER to enter from the north you have to ascend a stone's throw to reach the gate. It is very strong, with bastions all of living rock. In front of the gate is a great moat which you cross by way of a large wooden bridge.[a]

At the gate there are very tall guards who ask you what country you come from and where you are going. Also they wish to see the king's passports. Having been shown them, they lead you before the viceroy who asks the same questions. If you do not reply correctly nor have a valid passport, they shut you in prison or send you to the galleys. We showed our passports to the guards and to the viceroy who asked many things about Italy, and about Milan in particular. We told him as much as we knew.

We were allowed to pass and then went to the vicar to have the dimissory signed in order to say Mass. Then we went to the cathedral which is nearby, somewhat to one side of the city towards the east, on fairly high ground. It is a large church and is well administered. They make music with two choirs, both on the same side of the church. One is composed of singers, the other of various instruments, that is to say, harps, zithers, spinets and an organ with many pipes. It is all very different from the way we do it in Italy. They make a great melodious noise that can be heard from far off. Here they exhibit the Blessed Sacrament. It is seen by a great throng of people, for the Spanish are very devoted to this sacrament. I celebrated Mass and they gave me two *paoli* for alms.

While they are singing High Mass they feed twelve pilgrims just inside the door of the church at a table made ready for them. They make all the pilgrims go to the kitchen door and the cook gives each one a bowl of broth,

A *The present cathedral was begun in 1397, replacing an 11th-century building. The kitchen, together with the adjoining refectory is now part of the diocesan museum. The kitchen is square and has four fireplaces, one in each corner. Above each, fairly high up, is a squinch, which also acts as a chimney. This has been achieved by the ingenious device of building hollow squinches with an aperture at the bottom through which smoke can rise. The smoke then converged on a central chimney at the top of the tower.*

B *This well-known but wholly unhistorical narrative was widely popular in the Middle Ages. Entitled* Turpin's History of Charlemagne and Roland *it originally formed part of a larger work, the* Book of St James, *which appeared in 1139 or soon after. (* Turpini historia Karoli Magni et Rotholandi, *being Book 4 of the* Liber Sancti Jacobi, *see: Bédier, J.,* Les légendes épiques: Recherches sur la formation des chansons de geste, *Paris 1908-13, 3rd edition 1926-9, vol. 3, pp. 39 ff; also Meredith-Jones, C.,* Historia Karoli Magni et Rotholandi, ou chronique du Pseudo-Turpin, *Paris, 1936; Mâle, Émile,* Religious Art in France, the 12th century, *p. 491, notes 20 and 21, Princeton [Bollingen series x c : 1], 1978. For a full discussion of the* Liber Sancti Jacobi *see Williams, J. and Stones, A., (eds),* The Codex Calixtinus and the shrine of St James, *Tubingen, 1992.) The author of the* History *is unknown, though it purports to*

instead of thick vegetable soup, because in these parts they don't make it. When they all have their bowlful, they are made to stand in single file and go in procession through the church, carrying their bowl of soup. On reaching the table each one sits at his appointed place. Then they come with a large basket of bread and give one to each pilgrim. Next, another comes with a big cauldron of meat, and gives one piece to each; behind him is another who brings a slice of pork to each one; then finally they bring wine, and give a jug to each. Thus the ceremony is finished. Then in the evening they give the blessing of the Sacrament, with music, as they do in the morning, when it is exhibited.[a]

This is a truly outstanding city, graced with fine palaces and superb buildings. There are beautiful squares and fine monasteries of all kinds of religious Orders, with both monks and nuns. We toured the city for a space of four hours looking inside all these ancient buildings. We reached the district that lies between north and east where a large part of the city wall had fallen. They had built another some distance outside the old one. We asked why they had not rebuilt the wall in the same place. They replied that they had left it thus in memory of a miracle of St James of Galicia, which occurred in the time of Charlemagne. They said it happened in this way.[b]

Charlemagne, having taken the Holy Land in the company of Constantine I, and having won many other kingdoms was inclined to rest from war, for he did not wish to fight any longer. Having made this decision, on the very next night he saw in the sky a starry way beginning in Friesland and leading towards the German lands and Italy, then through France and Aquitaine. It passed onwards through Gascony, the Basque country and Navarre, then through Spain as far as Galicia. In that place there lay hidden until that time the body of St James the apostle. This vision he saw another three nights in succession, not understanding its meaning. Then, at the hour of midnight, at the time he was accustomed to seeing it, there appeared to him a man of fair aspect and yet not of the flesh, who said to him:

'What are you doing Charles, my son?'

'Who are you, O Sir?' replied Charles.

'I,' he said, 'am the apostle St James of Galicia, disciple of Christ, son of Zebedee, brother of St John, whom the Lord, through his ineffable grace on the Sea of Galilee,

have been written by Archbishop Turpin of Reims who, according to the Song of Roland, *fought (and died) beside the twelve peers of Charlemagne at Roncesvalles. The* Book of St James, *in which the* History *first appeared, seems to have been intended as a work of propaganda addressed to Compostellan pilgrims. It was written in France, perhaps prompted by the abbot of Cluny. It may have been intended to create a role for the French in the by-then flourishing cult of St James in which they had up to that time played only a minor part. The* History *makes the purely fictitious claims that Charlemagne made three expeditions to Spain (whereas he personally led only the one that ended in disaster at Roncesvalles), that he conquered the peninsula 'from one sea to the other', making the roads to Compostella safe for pilgrims, and that it was he who uncovered the apostle's tomb.*

deigned to choose to preach the gospel to these people. I am he whom Herod beheaded, whose body remains unrecognized in the country of Galicia because that kingdom is unworthily oppressed by the Saracens. Now I am astonished that you have not yet liberated my land, you who have subdued many kingdoms, cities and towns under your rule. Therefore I say to you that since the Lord has made you the most powerful among the rulers of the earth, so has he chosen you from among them all to prepare my path and to free my land from the hands of the Moabites and in due time will prepare a crown for your reward. The starry way you have seen, signifies that you have to go with a great army and drive out those perfidious people and open up the road. You will triumphantly uncover my sacred body, which lies in the furthest confines of Galicia. You are the first who will prepare the way for all people who will hasten to honour my remains.'

St James the apostle appeared thus to Charlemagne three times. After this Charles set out with a great army and, after crossing the Pyrenees, at once laid siege to the city of Pamplona, the capital and metropolis of Navarre. He stayed there three months without achieving his objective. Finally,

Fig. 47 *The 'French Gate', Pamplona.*

A *Laffi gives as his source the* Teatrum Vitæ Humanæ *by Luis de Granada (1504-88), a Spanish writer of devotional books.*

B *He died in 1516!*

C *He died in 1492!*

D *He died in 1493!*

E *For the life of Ignatius Loyola, see Brodrick, J.,* Saint Ignatius Loyola, *1956.*

seeing he was not able to take it and that every assault was in vain, the walls remaining impregnable, he prayed to God and St James the apostle that for the honour of his name and the exaltation of the Holy Faith, he might be given strength and grace to take the city. His prayer being done, suddenly the wall collapsed to its very foundations, revealing a great road to Charlemagne. He entered through the ruins with his whole army and captured the city. Those Saracens who turned to baptism were spared, those who refused were put to the sword. When these things reached the ears of other cities they surrendered to Charles and almost all the country paid tribute. This was the first time that the French crossed into Spain after the defeat at Roncesvalles.[a]

The second time the French entered Spain was in 1521 when Don Ferdinando was king.[b] That was in the time of Innocent VIII[c] and the Emperor Frederick III.[d] They came to besiege Pamplona, where Ignatius Loyola was installed with many companies of soldiers to withstand the besiegers. But because they were so hemmed in and because they did not see any hope of aid they were already thinking of surrender. However, Ignatius would not agree, exhorting them to resist the enemy until death. Then one day, when the French were making a vigorous attack on the city, he ran to the defence of a certain quarter where the fighting was fiercest. There he was wounded by a cannonball striking his right leg and, in the left leg by a stone which was dislodged from the wall by the force of the ball. Ignatius fell and, as the poet said, 'With the fall of but one, all fell,' because, dismayed by Ignatius' fall, they at once surrendered to the French. The latter, having captured Ignatius, took great care of him and sent him home. Out of this misfortune there came his vocation and he became a saint.[e]

After walking round the city and seeing what there was to see, we went to the inn, took our belongings and left Pamplona. We went through some hills, not very high, but the going was difficult. Beyond the hills we passed through a great forest, finally reaching Puente la Reina. It is about five very long and difficult leagues away. Here we passed the night. This is a very good place as it lies by a river and is sheltered by high hills. After taking a short walk through the town and seeing its fine buildings and churches we looked for an inn to lodge. But we could find nothing be-

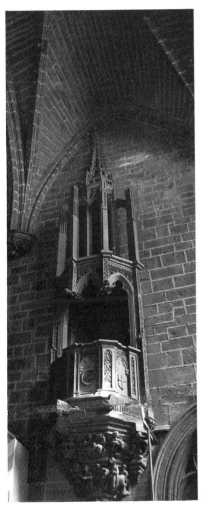

Fig. 48 *Lector's pulpit in the former refectory of the canons, part of the cathedral complex, Pamplona.*

cause the place was already full of people and there was nowhere for us. We had to make shift elsewhere. We looked for a lodging in many places but in vain. But then God, who never abandons anyone, reminded us that at the entrance to the town, at the distance of no more than a gunshot, there was a little chapel in the middle of the open road. We decided to go there in order to sleep inside. When we arrived we saw a peasant standing at a window looking at us. We begged him to give us lodging, promising to pay him however much he asked. The man, moved either by interest or compassion, came down, opened the door to us and made us very welcome, seeing we were dressed as priests. For truly the Spanish show a great regard for the Church and its clergy.

He led us into the house and wanted to give us bread. But we would not take it, because of the expense, since he was very poor, and we had already bought some. But he gave us good wine to drink and then we went to bed. This bed consisted of four heaps of vines spread on the ground and covered with a blanket. Thus we settled down as best we could. In the morning, half crippled, we went to the principal church to see if we could say Mass, but could find no one. But we received pardon through the Holy Sacrament and then crossed the bridge to follow the road to Estella, four leagues away.

This is a beautiful town*ᶠ* that lies on both sides of a great river. We crossed it by a great bridge, not very long but high. There are some fine large houses and monasteries, in particular the monastery of the Redemption where they provide charity to all pilgrims, consisting of bread and wine. In the *castello* they give alms of money to those pilgrims who are going to St James of Galicia. On leaving here we went to Urbiola, a distance of two leagues. This is a small place but has everything in abundance.

Outside the town [Estella] is a large and magnificent Benedictine monastery. It is very wealthy and seems like a town itself because it has a big surrounding wall and is very large. We entered the monastery and arrived in a splendid cloister embellished with sculpture, the like of which I believe I have never seen in all my days. Here there is a public university with a large number of students from different countries who study here. A brother who was passing with a group of the students, saw us and called to us. He asked

*The Benedictine monastery at
Irache is known to have existed in
the tenth century, and possessed
one of the oldest pilgrimage hos-
pitals along the route. It was once
famous for its hospitality to pilgrims. From 1569 until 1824 it
provided a university education.
Laffi's comments on its size and its
surrounding wall is a reminder
that it was formerly a Cistercian
community. That Order chose
spacious rural locations for its
houses so that they would be both
secluded and at the same time
large enough to be self-sufficient
in supplying their daily needs.
The Cistercian abbey at Gimont
was planned on similar lines.*

what country we came from and where we were going, and
many things about Italy, especially about the university of
Bologna. We described it to him to the best of our ability,
from what we knew about it. Finally, after various other
questions, he called the steward who led us to the refectory.
He himself came too, conversing with us. He had food
brought to us, while talking to the students about Italian
matters. They had come in great numbers to hear the
brother discoursing with us. Having finished eating we
thanked him and continued on our way.[a]

We passed by a field of young green beans and picked a
few. Then we came to a spring where we refreshed ourselves because it was very hot. We rested a while and then
continued towards Los Arcos, two leagues further. This is
the last town in the kingdom of Navarre, but the wind and
rain were so terrible we could travel no further. With God's
help we reached Los Arcos and sheltered there from the
rain while we dried our clothes. In the morning we went to
the main church to celebrate Mass and were given alms by

one of the canons. This is truly a well-fortified place, and well kept and there are plenty of things like fruit and vegetables in the main square, and good bread. We carried on towards Viana, four leagues away, passing through a very small place where we looked everywhere to buy wine and bread but could find none. From here we went to Viana, accompanied by hunger. On arrival we were much cheered up to see such a fine town with a beautiful church, so well ordered that it wanted for nothing. It has a splendid door with the most beautiful reliefs. Here we received the *passada* of bread and wine, and then continued to Logroño a distance of only one league.

This is the first city in the kingdom of Old Castile. One enters by a big bridge on the north side, in the middle of which stand the guards. They asked us our city and native land and where we were going and whether we had any contraband in our bundles. We replied no, and that we were going to Galicia. Whereupon they let us continue on our way as far as the city gate. Here the same thing happened and they let us enter. Once inside we went straight to the main square where we found they were holding a procession of the Most Holy Sacrament, which was done with truly great devotion and in an orderly manner. We followed

Fig. 51 *A doorway, known as the 'Puerto Especiosa' (1547), in the cloister of the Irache monastery. Above is an Assumption of the Virgin, which is flanked by s s. Benedict and Bernard.*

PAMPLONA TO BURGOS

it, and when it was over we went through the city looking at the palaces and churches which are splendid.

This is really a very grand city, very beautiful, rich and comfortable, with an abundance of everything. It is situated in a plain. Near its walls on the northern side, as I said, runs a great river, flowing from west to east.[a] Having toured round a good deal and seen many fine monasteries of monks and nuns, we arrived at a great gate leading out of the city. On leaving by this way one enters a kind of large amphitheatre,[b] an octagon with very big balconies all round. Thus people can see well when they hold festivals. It can hold many thousands of people. They put on spectacles such as hunting wild bulls, lions, horses, bears and wild boars. Sometimes they have carnivals, pageants, plays and suchlike entertainments.

We left the amphitheatre by a different gate and came to a fine, broad street entirely paved, with two rows of very tall trees on either side. They gave us a pleasant and much welcome shade. It is half a mile long and at the end stands a convent of St Teresa, which is very handsome and well-provided. On the left side of the street is a fountain which discharges water in great quantities. It runs through many gardens and orchards making them extremely fertile. But as it was late we returned to our lodging, buying bread and wine and everything else we needed. This was not to be wondered at because an inn in Spain provides nothing but sleeping accommodation. You have to buy everything else going here and there through the city, because he who sells one thing may not sell something else you need. In the morning we went to the cathedral to say Mass because it was the feast day of St Anthony of Padua.[c]

That done, we left the town and made for Navarrete, two leagues away. This is a fortified town, like a boat in outline, and is situated on the top of a hill. It is very strong and is surrounded by stout walls. It has a large, splendid church, which is well maintained and well administered. We left the town and bought some fruit so we could refresh ourselves later at some spring or other. But we walked for a while without finding any water, with a fierce sun beating down on us. Eventually, by God's will, we came to an olive tree in the middle of a field, which we had seen from some miles away. Here we stopped in its shade and then carried on towards Nájera, three leagues away.

The Najerilla.

This is one of the finest towns to be seen in this region. It lies in a plain and has a broad river[a] flowing through it. It is spanned by a fine bridge connecting two parts of the town on the west side. There is a very steep hill, all of bare rock, which overshadows the town in such a way that half of it is sheltered from rain and sun, except until about mid-day. It is really a beautiful place and well supplied with everything. They are busy all day constructing many buildings, together with churches. There are three squares, one on the near side of the bridge, the others across the bridge to the west. When we rose in the morning we bought bread and wine because, particularly in Spain, you should never leave a town without them. From here we began our jour-

The sound of cock-crow still
echoes through the cathedral
even today, for a pair of white
fowls are kept in an elaborate
coop, with a metal grill, on the
wall of the south transept. They
commemorate a famous local
legend (see below). A French pilgrim, Guillaume Manier, from
Carlepont in Picardy, passed
through Santo Domingo in
1726. He wrote in his Pèlerinage d'un Paysan Picard
*that every pilgrim was given
two or three white feathers to
wear in his hat, to ensure
St James's protection. Laffi's
account of the birds' behaviour
is much embroidered – they are
changed, nowadays at least,
every two or three weeks. See
Bonnault d'Houët, Xavier de,*
Le pèlerinage d'un paysan
picard, *Montdidier, 1890;
reprinted in* Mémoires de la
Société nationale des Anti-
quaires de France, *vol. 111,
pp. 117-28, Paris, 1893.*

———

Fig. 52 *The hen-house in
the cathedral of Sto Domingo de
la Calzada. Live fowls are behind
the bars. The manacles hanging
on the left are thank-offerings
of prisoners released
by the Moors.*

———

ney to Santo Domingo de la Calzada, climbing the great hill
which overlooks Nájera. Beyond it we arrived in a plain
where there were many fields. Eventually we came to the
beginning of a road.

Here we found a woman weeping bitterly who begged us
to go with her. We were a bit suspicious because we had
been told about women in these parts who, under some pre-
text or other – either children needing baptism or men dying and asking for confession – lead travellers to where men
are lying in wait to assassinate them. We were, as I say, suspicious and afraid to follow her. But we were persuaded by
her floods of tears, and followed her into a nearby field,
where she had two donkeys stuck in the mud in a deep bog.
We gave her a hand and after much time and effort dragged
them out. Whereupon she began laughing and crying all
at once, no longer from sorrow but from joy. She thanked
us profusely giving us a thousand blessings. Then we continued on our way to Santo Domingo de la Calzada, four
long leagues away.

This is a fine city, though small, with a noble square and
fine monasteries of both monks and nuns. As soon as we
reached the square we went to the cathedral by the side
door. Just inside we saw the cock and hen which are shut in
an iron bird-cage on the left as you enter. As we entered the
church, wearing our pilgrim's garb, they began to crow with
joy and make a great to-do. They do this to all pilgrims. We
asked the sacristan for some feathers, which he gave us and,
out of piety, we brought them home with us. These creatures eat only what is given to them by pilgrims going to
Galicia. It must be bread – and only bread that they have
found for the love of God, for if it be bread that has been
purchased, they will have nothing to do with it and would
rather die of hunger. So, when there are no pilgrims passing by, there is a woman who looks after them. She goes
through the city dressed as a pilgrim, begging for alms, and
thus they are provided for. We gave them bread which
they took readily. There was a great crowd of people watching them take the bread and crow about it, being so joyful.
They are like this to all pilgrims who come here. Towns-
people and strangers, seeing pilgrims arrive, all come directly into the church, drawn by curiosity. As a consequence
they provide great charity to all the monasteries and also
throughout the town.[b]

At the high altar we were granted indulgence. Above the altar is the gibbet of that pilgrim, of whom I shall tell you shortly. Then we looked round the cathedral which is very fine and so majestic, because it is very old. Next we walked round the town. On passing through the square we met once more the woman with the two asses that we had extracted from the bog. She greeted us very warmly and gave us a loaf of bread, which we accepted willingly, thanking her for it.

Then we left by the west gate where there is a large and splendid friary of the Observantine Franciscans.[a] It has a beautiful church that is well cared for. While we were looking at the paintings in the church the sacristan approached us to say that he wanted to close it because it was the dinner hour. We told him he should close it whenever he wished since he was in charge. As we left the church he asked us what country we were from and where we were going. When we told him he went on to say that if we waited until the friars had dined we should be given dinner too. So we waited until the friars had finished and then the sacristan came and led us to the refectory and gave us dinner. We were served at table by two novices, assigned to the task by the superior. After the meal we thanked them, and were given in addition plenty of bread and fish, since it was Saturday. Then they accompanied us to the door with many expressions of kindness and courtesy.

Not far away we found a little old chapel where we stopped. On going inside we saw on one side of the altar an inscription that told of those three pilgrims going to St James of Galicia, and the miracle of the cock and hen. The place where the chapel had been built was where one of the three pilgrims had been wrongly hanged. It happened in this way.

In the year 1090 a husband and wife with their son, of Greek nationality from the city of Thessalonica, were going to St James of Galicia. On reaching Santo Domingo de la Calzada, 240 miles from St James they stopped, tired out from travel. They found an inn and stayed two days. The innkeeper's daughter fell wildly in love with the young pilgrim and during the night went to his room to make her wanton desires known to him. He, covered with bashfulness on hearing a young girl make known her passion so shamelessly, rebuked her want of chastity and vehemently scolded her, saying he cared nothing for her. This is something which merely arouses wrath in a woman's bosom. Her chagrin caused the girl's love to turn to anger, which was transformed into a deep rage seething in her breast. She was determined to take revenge by means of a certain stratagem which her anger inspired. She took a silver cup and went quietly again to the young man's room where he had once more fallen asleep. She hid the cup in his bag and returned quietly to her own room for the rest of the night, delighted at having avenged the affront she had been given, and was congratulating herself with the prospect to come when sleep overtook her.

When day came the pilgrims left the town. The innkeeper's daughter, who had waited impatiently for the moment to take her revenge, pretended to look for the cup she had hidden, knowing it could not be found except in the poor lad's bag. She began to bewail the loss of the cup, accusing the three pilgrims. So her father, believing his daughter's words, set out in pursuit, taking constables with him. Meanwhile the three, with no thought except of safely reaching their destination, were overtaken and stopped. The officers of the law opened their bags, searched them thoroughly and found the cup in the young man's bag. On discovering the 'theft' they let the old parents go and took the son back to the town. Here, he was straight away sentenced to death as a thief and was hanged.

Fig. 53 *'Le pendu dépendu'.*
Engraving by Francesco di
Giovanni Benvenuto, 1519.
(Biblioteca Nazionale,
Florence.)

The wretched father and mother, heart-broken at the loss of their only son, continued on their way to St James of Galicia. Before the altar of the holy apostle they commended their souls and that of their son to God and to the apostle. They wept bitterly for he was their only son, who would have been their hope and mainstay in their old age. Then, having finished their devotions, they set off for their homeland, consoled by having achieved their desire but desolate at having lost their only son. They reached the city of Astorga where there are two roads, one that goes directly to Santo Domingo de la Calzada and another, to the right, going to Valladolid. The poor old man, in order not to face once again the sight of their son which aroused such grief

in their hearts, wanted to take the way to Valladolid. However, after his wife had pleaded with him, they returned the way they had come. When they came to the place where their son was hanging they found him still alive! When he saw his parents he called out to them, saying, 'No more tears! By the grace of God, the Blessed Virgin and St James I am yet living, for they are supporting me in the air! Go, mother, to the judge and tell him that my innocence has kept me alive and that he orders me to be set free and restored to you.'

His mother did as she was bid, leaving her husband there. She came before the magistrate just as he was sitting down to table. She begged him for her son, saying they had found him still alive because he was innocent. But the magistrate only laughed and turned to the woman, still laughing, and said, 'Oh, how you are mistaken, my good lady, your son is no more alive than the two fowls on this dish.' Oh, wonder of wonders! Oh, the might of the Lord! No sooner had the magistrate uttered these words, than the two birds, a cock and a hen, sprang up from the dish and began to crow and cluck. The magistrate, witnessing the miracle, rose from the table in wonder and amazement. He left the house with the woman, calling on various clergy and citizens to accompany him. They all went to the place where the lad was hanging and, seeing that he was well and cheerful, restored him to his parents. They, well-satisfied and joyful, returned to Greece, their native land.

Then the magistrate returned home and, with all those who were present, took the cock and hen and carried them into the church with great solemnity. He put them in an iron cage where, as I told you earlier, everyone can see them. Such marvels testify to the great power of God. The two creatures each live for seven years because God has ordained that that is their span of life. At the end of seven years, before they die, the hen lays two eggs from which are hatched two chicks, one a cock, the other a hen. They are the same colour and the same size as their parents; and this happens in the church every seven years. What is so astonishing is that all the citizens, also visitors and pilgrims passing through, take feathers from the cock and hen and yet they never have any missing. I can confirm that this is so because I myself have seen them and carry some of these very feathers with me. The birds are as white as snow and

Fig. 54 *Christians giving thanks to St Dominic of Silos after their release from captivity by the Moors. Authentic fetters and manacles hang from the wall. A 13th-century relief (sculptor unknown) in the cloister of the monastery of Silos. (Courtesy of the Abadia Benedictina, Silos.)*

This legend is widely known and exists in different versions. It owes something to the Old Testament, story of Joseph and Benjamin (Gen. 44, 1-12). Various saints, including Sto Domingo, have been made the boy's saviour. The Book of St James *sets the story in Toulouse in 1090 and makes the innkeeper an Albigensian heretic, who is hanged when found out. In that account the pilgrims come from Germany. The subject is represented all along the pilgrimage roads and is sometimes treated as a cycle of scenes, especially in the stained glass of French and Italian churches. It occurs in the thirteenth-century song book, the* Cantigas de Santa Maria, *compiled by Alfonso the Wise, (where the boy's saviour is the Virgin), in pilgrim's songs, and is the subject of an Italian miracle play (Anon.,* Rappresentatione duno miracolo di tre Peregrini che andavano a sancto Iacopo di Galitia, *Florence, 1519. Text in* Emiliani-Guidici, P., Storia del teatro in Italia, *1860).*

B *St Dominic of the Highway.*

C *Domingo García, after whom the town is named, was Spanish, not Italian. He was born in the village of Viloria de Rioja, some ten miles away, probably in 1019 or 1020. As a young man he chose the monastic life but later abandoned it and became the disciple of the bishop of Ostia until the latter's death in 1044. He settled as a hermit in some deserted woodland close to the River Oca, near the road to Compostella. He devoted the rest of his life to passing pilgrims. An early document describes him as a 'nurse, doctor,*

so beautiful. One can no longer say what colour they might have been before they died that first time, that is to say, when they were cooked for the magistrate's table. The innkeeper and his daughter were punished according to their deserts. On the very spot where the young man was hanged they built a chapel dedicated to St James.[a]

This town is called Santo Domingo de la Calzada or, in Italian, San Domenico della Salicata,[b] because it is the place where a certain Blessed Dominic, an Italian, is buried. He came to these parts in the year 1050 with Gregory, bishop of Ostia, a saintly man, who was sent by the Pope at the request of the Navarrese in Spain. They sought some spiritual remedy to free them from a terrible plague that afflicted the kingdom of Navarre. The country was full of locusts which ate and destroyed all the fruits of the earth, so that the Navarrese people were reduced to a sorry state. They besought the Pope for some kind of help and remedy. He sent them this saintly bishop who, by his example, preaching, prayers, good works, alms-giving and penances brought many people to a better life. When their sins ended, so too did the plague.

The blessed Dominic stayed with the holy bishop until his death, whereupon he decided to remain in this place and do penance here. He chose it because it was far from human habitation. Moreover there was, in those days, a great forest here frequented by thieves and murderers who robbed pilgrims going to St James of Galicia, taking advantage of this difficult stretch of the way. Here he built a small cell for his dwelling and a little chapel in honour of the Blessed Virgin. He then began to clear the whole forest, cutting down and burning the scrub and trees where those evil-doers used to lurk. He built a fine, level road, paved with stone, so long, so splendid and so well-known that henceforth the saint was named after it. The same name was also given to the town that was later built here, where the cathedral church, also named after him, holds his tomb.

In addition to this Dominic built a very fine hospice to lodge pilgrims going to St James of Galicia. While it was being built another St Dominic, from Silos, came to see him. The two saints greeted each other with great affection and kindness. St Dominic of Silos praised the splendid highway and other works that his namesake had undertaken. The latter was a man who subjected himself to severe penances

*cook, bricklayer and architect,'
skills which he put to good use.
He built a bridge over the river
(which still exists though many
times restored), founded a hospital, and repaired the road over a
distance of some twenty miles. In
1098 he began building a church
on land donated by Alfonso VI.
It stood on the site of the present
church which acquired the status
of cathedral in 1232. St Dominic
of the Highway (Sp. calzada)
died in 1109 and is buried in the
cathedral in a magnificent tomb
(1513). His various undertakings
were the nucleus out of which the
town grew. (See Ubieto Arteta,
Agustín, Notas sobre el patri-
monio calceatense en los siglos
XII y XIII, Logroño, 1978; and
by the same author 'Apuntes para
la biografía de Santo Domingo de
la Calzada', Revista Berceo,
no.82, pp.25-36, Logroño, 1972.)*

D *A community of monks was already established at Silos in the
tenth century and adopted the rule
of St Benedict in 954. But the
monastery declined from the later
tenth century as a result of the
ravages of the formidable Mos-
lem military leader Al-Mansur
(d.1002). Dominic became abbot
in 1041 and was a powerful influence in restoring its fortunes,
spiritual and material, until
his death in 1073. He was subsequently made its titular saint.
Mementoes of his activities in
securing the release of prisoners
held by the Moors may be seen in
the cloister. See Fig.54, p.132.*

E *The parentage of St Dominic, see
Vicaire, M.-H., Histoire de Saint
Dominique, 1957: English trans-
lation, 1964.*

and self-discipline and lived for many years performing
such devout exercises. He died in the Lord and was buried
in the above-mentioned place. Soon afterwards they built
the magnificent monument described above, where I went
to see the cock and hen. Then the town was built, which
adopted and still retains the name of Santo Domingo de la
Calzada. The saint died on the twelfth of May, 1060.[c]

Saint Dominic of Silos stayed a few days with his namesake of Calzada and then returned home. There he built a
monastery of the Order of St Benedict, where he later died
after becoming its abbot. He had wrought many miracles
during his life and even after his death he was remarkable
for having secured the release of great numbers of Christians imprisoned by the Moors. These Christians, on commending themselves to the mercy of St Dominic found
themselves back in Christian lands. They left their chains
and other irons of their servitude at the gate of the monastery as tokens of their freedom, grateful to God as its
author and to St Dominic as His intermediary. It is wonderful to see so many chains and fetters that the liberated
prisoners left at the monastery. There is a Spanish saying
that goes: 'All the fetters of St Dominic of Silos would not
be enough for you.'[d]

When he died he was buried in the monastery. There was
a certain Donna Giovanna Baza who prayed at his tomb,
asking the saint to intercede with God to give her safe de-
livery of the child that she carried in her womb. While she
was praying the saint appeared to her in person and gave
her reassurance about the blessed son she was about to
bear. The son was called Dominic, after his patron and ad-
vocate, St Dominic of Silos, and later became the patriarch,
St Dominic, the founder of the Order of Preachers.[e]

We left the chapel – where the pilgrim was hanged – and
continued on our way to Grañón, two leagues away. This is
a small and very poor village. We spent the night there and
early next morning carried on to Redecilla del Camino, a
small place. Here we asked permission to say Mass but were
not allowed to because we had not had the dimissory signed
at Santo Domingo de la Calzada. However we continued to
Castildelgado where, with God's aid, we said Mass. It is a
small place, but pleasant and prosperous. We then set out
for Belorado, three leagues away, and thence to Villafranca
Montes de Oca, another three leagues. This is a prosperous

The hospice was founded in 1380 by Doña Juana Manuel, the wife of Henry 11, king of Castile, and was known as the Queen's Hospice. It was one of the most highly regarded along this section of the road. In the middle of the kitchen was a square fireplace around which were two banks of seats where pilgrims could warm themselves while drying their clothes. On the first floor were dormitories, an infirmary and a chapel.

B *San Juan de Ortega.*

C *Like St Dominic of the Highway, St John of Ortega (1080-1163) devoted the latter part of his life to improving the path of the Compostellan pilgrim through various building works. After making the pilgrimage to Jerusalem he returned to his home ground and set about building a church, a hospice, a stretch of roadway and several bridges. The east end of the present church has Romanesque features dating from the second half of the twelfth century, which are the work of St John. His tomb is in the church.*

place of some size, situated at the foot of a mountain, with its houses partly on the mountain and partly in the plain. They give great charity to pilgrims here, in particular in the hospice, where the food is exceedingly good.[a]

We stayed here for our meal and then rested, since it was midday and very hot. We then set out to climb the steep mountain. Beyond, we found ourselves in a broad plain of meadowland for the space of four leagues, without a single dwelling. In the meadows we found huge mushrooms of unbelievable size, as big as a large straw hat. We picked two of them, one for each of us. Once through the fields we came to a monastery of the fathers of St John,[b] whose body is preserved in a marble coffin in the monastery. The fathers are wealthy and are very charitable to pilgrims. After receiving indulgence at the altar of St John we went on to a nearby village called Villanueva, where we spent the night. We were well satisfied, what with our mushrooms, which were now cooked, and good bread and wine. Then we continued on our way to Burgos, five leagues away. In all that stretch of road there is no more then one very small village.[c]

ACROSS THE MESETA
Burgos to León

Burgos stands on the banks of the River Arlanzón. It was founded in 884 and chosen as the capital of the kingdoms of Castile and León on their union in 1037. This took place under Ferdinand 1, king of Castile, of whom it was said, 'he loved poor pilgrims and took great care to shelter them.' Burgos was once renowned for the number of its hospices. The cathedral was founded in 1221. In spite of some insensitive restorations in the eighteenth century it remains an outstanding example of Spanish Gothic architecture and sculpture. Important additions were made in the fifteenth century. Under the crossing is buried Rodrigo Diaz de Bivar (1026-99), called El Cid Campeador, the brilliant soldier whose exploits are the subject of Spain's national epic.

BURGOS IS A TRULY SPLENDID CITY. IT IS BIG and is the metropolis of Old Castile where the king once had his court. It lies in a fine, spacious plain through which runs a delightful river. The cathedral is very old. It is of average size, but its facade is truly superb: from the topmost point to its foundations it is all carved in relief and is structurally magnificent, with paintings that have no equal. In a word, the building is wholly sumptuous and regal.[a]

On the south side stands the archiepiscopal palace where we went to have the dimissory signed. Then we went to the Augustinian Friars to say Mass. We said it at the altar of Santo Cristo, called the Crucifix of Burgos, one of three crucifixes made by Nicodemus. Indeed, this holy image would move the very stones to compassion, were they capable of feeling. It is so well made and has such a mournful expression that when people set eyes on it, it draws tears of pity. One cannot deny that this is the true and real likeness of Christ, so lacerated by the scourge that his human aspect is lost. St Nicodemus, inspired with divine love and contemplating at all hours the death of the Lord, had his likeness imprinted in his heart and before his eyes. As I said, he made three crucifixes, all life-size, though of different forms. They are today most deeply venerated. The one at Burgos I have seen with my own eyes, to my very great joy. It is treated with great reverence. I will tell you briefly how this image came to Burgos as Tomaso Errera, Lucio Sicolo and Giovanni Marquesi have described it.

In 1119 there was a merchant of Burgos, who had to go on a journey. Before leaving he went to the church of the Augustinian Hermits and asked them if they would pray to God for him that his journey might prosper. He said that on his return he would bring some precious gift for them. The merchant departed on his journey, which turned out favourably and the Hermits thus fulfilled what they had promised. The merchant returned home and – as so often happens, when one has received a service one forgets to give thanks for it – he forgot the promise he had made to the Hermits. However, while he was still at sea a violent tempest blew up. So he commended himself wholeheartedly to God, whereupon the storm subsided. Then he was deeply ashamed for having forgotten the promise he had made to the Hermits. While he remained plunged in thought he saw floating over the waters a wooden chest. He immediately sent someone to recover it. When he opened it he saw inside another chest made of glass within which was the image of Christ. It was stretched out like a corpse, with arms and hands folded over the body, as if it had just been detached from the cross. All the joints were articulated, and the feet were transfixed by two nails, one bigger than the other. It was covered with a white garment from waist to knees.

When this holy cross reached Burgos, the home-town of the merchant, they say that the bells of the church of St Augustine rang of their own accord for joy, for it was here that it was to be housed. A few years later the bishop claimed that the image belonged in his own church, but this was opposed by the Augustinians. So the image was put

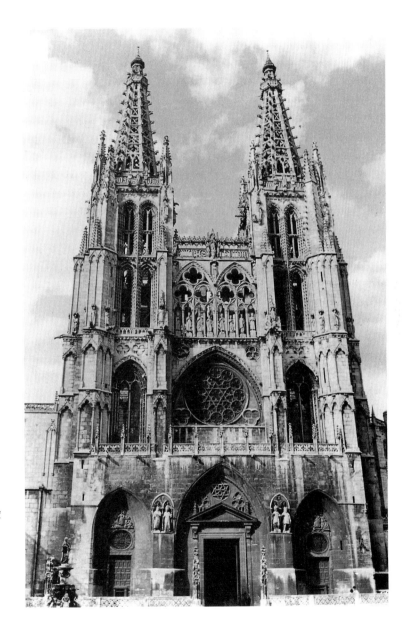

Fig. 55 *Burgos in the mid-17th century, from an etching by Mathaus Merian in* the Theatrum Europeum. *There are several inaccuracies in the representation of the cathedral.*

Fig. 56 *Burgos cathedral, west front. Much decorative sculpture formerly surrounding the portals was removed during restorations in the 18th century.*

BURGOS TO LEÓN

The famous effigy of Christ, formerly in the monastery of the Augustinian Friars, was moved to the cathedral in 1835, where it has its own chapel. It was made about the thirteenth century or earlier and owes its lifelike appearance to the use of ox-hide to resemble human flesh and natural hair for the scalp and beard. Its head and limbs are articulated. It belongs to a class of image, not uncommon in medieval and earlier Church history, that was specially revered for its quasi-human character and apparent power to work miracles. The 'Christ of Burgos' was said to sweat and to shed blood; some even maintained that it was shaved every week and had its finger and toe nails cut (So Guillaume Manier was told in 1726-7. He gives a very detailed description of the chapel. See Bonnault d'Houët, op. cit., Ch.10, n.4). It is mentioned in the songs and ballads of Compostellan pilgrims and is thus well known along their roads. Nicodemus was one of those who helped remove Christ's body from the cross (John, 19:39). He was never canonized.

Fig. 57   *The 'Christ of Burgos' (detail), 13th century.*

on a she-mule, which had its eyes blindfolded and had no one to guide it, so that God should send it where he willed. But the mule, after a long journey round the town returned to the place where it had started. Not pleased about this, the bishop had the image removed and brought into his own church. But the next night the sacred image miraculously returned to its original place.[a]

In this church I celebrated Mass, as I said, at the altar of the sacred crucifix. After Mass we went to the sacristy and deposited the utensils. The sacristan gave us bread that had

Fig. 58 *A carved walnut panel on the church door of the Hospital del Rey, an example of late Spanish Gothic art, possibly by Felipe Vigarny (d. 1543). It represents a family of pilgrims on their way to Santiago.*

been blessed, which the fathers dispense – an act of great holiness. The bread is very beneficial for a variety of complaints, in particular fever. There is a fountain here which is called the 'Fountain of the Crucifix' and which gives a very sweet water. They dispense it as a spiritual draught.

After we had seen a few other things in the city we left, walking a quarter of a mile beside a river on a paved road with many trees on each side. At the end of it we came to a hospice, which for its size seemed like a city in itself. I don't think there is another like it in Spain. It holds two thousand people. They give much charity to pilgrims and treat

A *The 'King's Hospice', or Hospital del Rey, was founded by Alfonso VIII in 1195 expressly for poor pilgrims. The charity it provided was proverbial. According to a German pilgrim in 1495, 'They give you food and drink until you are sated' (Herman Künig von Vach. See Häbler, Konrad, Das Walfartsbuch des Hermannus Künig von Vach und die Pilgerreisen der Deutschen nach Santiago de Compostela, Strasbourg, 1899; English translation: Durant, John; Confraternity of Saint James, London, 1993). Linguists were in residence so that confessions could be heard in several tongues. Pilgrims of many nationalities lie in the adjoining cemetery. Laffi's figure of two thousand is merely an indication of its great size and is not meant to be taken literally.*

them very well as regards eating and sleeping. There is a person who accompanies a friar of the Franciscan Order of Observants and who speaks all languages. They are in charge of this hospice, which is called the Hospice of the King. They recognise no other superior but the king himself.[a]

We left the hospice and had not gone a league before we came to a small town called Hornillos del Camino. Outside the place is a Carthusian monastery. It is very large and, being some distance from the road, they have built an outhouse on the public way where they give a *passada* of bread and wine to passing pilgrims, so that they do not spend their time going to the monastery itself. From here onwards it is very easy to lose one's way because one sees nothing but empty, sandy plain. So, for the benefit of poor pilgrims, I shall give directions to keep them on the right road so they do not get lost. On first arriving in this sandy waste – or any others of the same kind – when you come to two or three roads and want to know which is the right one, you will find pilgrims have made two or three heaps of stones by the side of whichever road is the right one. Likewise, on reaching a wood where there may also be two or three ways, to know which is the right one you will see that pilgrims strip the bark from two or three trees with the tip of their stave to show that this is the way to follow. In an uninhabited place where there may be two or three roads they set up a cross of stone or wood. On one arm they write the name of the town towards which the road goes that way and on the other arm the name of the town where that road goes.

I should like also to explain to needy pilgrims something very useful to them, which demonstrates the great charity that they extend in Spanish cities and other places in the kingdom. When a pilgrim arrives at a place where there is no hospice he may go to the local constable, whom they call the *alguazil*, in other words the justice, to appeal to him. The constable will then call one of his men who will lead the pilgrim to an inn that has a good bed. Also, if he needs bread or wine they will give it to him without hesitation. Whatever the pilgrim needs, if he asks the constable, that they will provide without any question. If he falls ill he may ask those who have horses to give him bread and wine, and then take him on horseback to the nearest village, or carry on to another if need be, until they come to one that has a good hospital where the sick man may be taken care of.

Continuing on our way we met, at the outhouse that I mentioned above, three Germans who were going to Galicia. We joined them, walking together the whole day across the great plain. It was scorched, not only by the sun, but by swarms of locusts which had destroyed everything. One could see neither tree nor grass of any kind. Nor are there even rocks, for everything is sand. There were so many of these accursed locusts that one could walk only with difficulty. At every step they rose in the air in clouds so dense that you could hardly see the sky. This continued for six leagues, from Burgos to Hontanas. With God's help we crossed this deserted waste land and reached the village of Hontanas. It lies hidden in the valley of a little river, so that you scarcely see it until you have reached it. Moreover it is small, wretched and poor. There are ten or a dozen huts, roofed with straw, that look like winter refuges from the snow, though they are occupied by shepherds. They have a strong palisade round the huts to guard against wolves which come at night to attack them. These creatures are so famished they even eat one another. There are so many of them that you see them in packs, like flocks of sheep, both in the daytime and at night. So whenever you want to cross this desert you must do it in the middle of the day when the shepherds are out with their huge dogs. Only then can you pass safely. Having reached this wretched place by the evening, we ate a little bread with garlic which the German gave us, and drank a little wine. Then we went to bed on the ground because there was nowhere else. We were allowed to stay in one of the huts, after we had paid for our lodging in advance.

In the morning we rose early but these Spanish people told us that we ought not to leave too early because the wolves would kill us. We should stay as late as possible until all shepherds had gone out into the fields, just as they do in the desert near Burgos. So we waited a little and then continued to Castrojeriz, two leagues on, the road everywhere covered with those accursed locusts. They eat not only fruit and vegetation but vines and even trees. It is pitiful to behold because not only people die of hunger but also beasts because they cannot find pasture, all having been consumed by these creatures. We came upon a poor French

The Puente Fitero.

Fig. 59 *Christian against Moor (the long shield is the Christian's, the round shield, the Moor's: see also p. 114). Church of St James, soffit of west facade, 1150-85. Carrión de los Condes.*

pilgrim lying in the road. He was dying, and was all covered with locusts. It seems God must have sent us to help his soul, since hardly had we confessed him than he died. Those cruel little creatures had begun to devour him, and while we stayed with him we had great difficulty in protecting ourselves from their voracious appetites. Dead as he was we covered his face and hands with sand, so that the locusts might not eat him, and then continued on to Castrojeriz.

On reaching the town we went to find the priest and told him there was a dead pilgrim one league away. He promised to send someone to fetch him. Then we left the town, which is a large, well-fortified place lying between two hills, and having an abundance of everything. We crossed a big bridge, and went up a steep hill, after which we came to a great, wide plain. It is completely barren. In the middle you cross a big bridge called the Ponte della Mulla.[a] We crossed it, continuing over the plain under a fearful sun, always with those evil locusts, until we arrived, with God's help, at Fromista, fifteen miles away. Here we stayed the night.

This place is so big it is like a city, but there is a terrible famine since, because of the locusts, they have been able to harvest neither wheat, the vines, nor fruit, nor anything. It is wretched to see these places so desolate because of these creatures. At night all the inhabitants of the area go out through the town with wooden clubs and kill the locusts which collect under the walls during the day, covering them so that they appear to be painted black. At night they fall to the ground because of the cold, and they then come and kill them. If they did not do this they would indeed have abandon the land, and the very town itself.

Here in the church we saw a beautiful miracle wrought by the Holy Sacrament. There was a certain Fernando (which in Tuscan would be called Ferdinando) who was approaching death. He had been excommunicated on account of a debt but, having paid it, he did not obtain absolution from his excommunication, nor did he confess the sin. Having paid the debt he considered himself free to receive the sacrament. As I said, he was on the point of death and so he asked for communion. The parish priest brought the sacrament to his bedside, as is the custom with the sick, but when he went to take the wafer in his hand to give communion to the sick man it stuck to the paten so firmly that

B *Luis de Granada,* op. cit. *on p. 122; also, same author,* Cathe, *vol. 2.*

C *The story of the miraculous paten and wafer is known in more than one version. This curious object was kept in the church from 1453 and was greatly venerated, especially by pilgrims. It is no longer there but is commemorated in a street name, the* Calle del Milagro, *the Street of the Miracle, which leads to the church.*

D *San Zoilo.*

E *Santa Maria de las Tiendas.*

he could not loosen it either with his finger-nail or with a knife, and it became all bloody. The priest, amazed, questioned the sick man who remembered his excommunication and confessed. He then took communion with another consecrated wafer. The wafer attached to the paten was taken into the church as it was, and is still preserved there with great veneration.[b] It is shown to anyone who wishes to see it, in particular to pilgrims who pass that way.[c]

When we left the church, we walked round the town until it was evening. We took bread and wine and had supper with our Germans, who had also been round the town, selling parchment figures of saints, which they had with them.

Next morning we continued on our way, leaving early and walking to Carrión de los Condes, four leagues away. This is an ordinary village, very well supplied with goods, and there are a number of religious houses of friars, particularly Franciscans. Leaving Carrión, we came to a large monastery[d] where they give pilgrims a *passada* of bread and wine. After this we passed over great tracts of deserted country where there were swarms of locusts, so many that we were barely able to walk. Then we came to Calzadilla de la Cueza, four leagues away, but since it was night when we arrived we could not find any lodging, so we had to sleep in the open air. However we managed to have a cheerful night with the Germans who were travelling with us. In the morning we rose early, wasting no time getting dressed. A short distance from the village where we had spent the night we came to a very large and wealthy hospice called Gran Cavaliere.[e] Here they give pilgrims a *passada* of bread and wine and cheese, of which there is plenty in this region because of the many herds. They also gave us cottage cheese (*ricotta*) and a loaf of bread each, as well as something to drink. Then we walked to a village called San Giovanni, two leagues away, and then to Sahagún, another two leagues.

At Sahagún the walls were covered with so many locusts that it made a pitiful sight. When we entered the town, we found women sweeping them away and killing them with wooden bats. We spent some time walking round the town, curious to see it. Among the religious houses there are two which are particularly rich and handsome, one Benedictine and the other the Observantine Franciscans. We went to the monastery of the Benedictines to see the refectory,

BURGOS TO LEÓN

The Benedictine abbey was one of the greatest in Spain in the Middle Ages, but is now a ruin. It was founded in 904 and became a dependency of Cluny in 1080. From that time it exerted a strong French influence, not always welcomed by the Spanish. The thirteenth-century church of the former Franciscan monastery, called 'La Peregrina', stands on a hill in the southern quarter of Sahagún overlooking the city. It owes its name to a seventeenth-century image of the Virgin in pilgrim's garb, in the role of their protectress.

which is such that I cannot believe any other could be finer. It has a vaulted ceiling of carved wood which is most magnificent and worth seeing by anyone. The monks gave us supper and treated us with great esteem.[a]

After we had thanked them we went to the Franciscan house to pick up the Germans, who had gone there to sell their parchment saints to the friars. Then we continued onwards to Burgo Ranero, four very long leagues away. After we had gone some three leagues we came across a dead pilgrim. Two wolves had begun to eat his body, so we chased them off and continued towards Burgo Ranero. When we arrived there it was evening. We went to see the priest and asked him to go and recover the body. Then we went to an inn, but it was such a poor one that we had to sleep on the floor, for the inhabitants of the village are all herdsmen, who live in huts roofed with straw. When we rose next morning we went on to Mansilla de las Mulas, four leagues away, and then another three leagues to León, which we reached about midday.

Fig. 60 *'La Peregrina': the Virgin with the accoutrements of a pilgrim. Her cape carries scallop shells. In her right hand she holds a staff from which a calabash hangs. The work of Luisa Roldán (c. 1656-1704). Sahagún.*

Fig. 61 *The fortifications of León, originally Roman, were restored by Alfonso v, king of León, in the 11th century, after the city had fallen to the Moors. The present walls were built by Alfonso xi in 1324. They retain vestiges of their Roman origins.*

────

A *The Gothic cathedral (1258-c. 1303), admired by Laffi, is especially remarkable for its stained glass.*

B *The Bernesga.*

C *The former monastery of St Mark was originally a poorhouse for pil-*

grims funded by royalty. It was taken over by a Spanish military Order, the Order of the Knights of Santiago, soon after their foundation in 1170. Like the Templars and Hospitallers in Spain they took an active part in the Reconquest, to drive the Moors out of the peninsula. The monastery was well known for taking good care of pilgrims. The facade of the adjoining church (1533-41) is decorated with scallop shells, the symbol of the Compostellan pilgrimage.

D *The image known as the Virgin of the 'Camino', reputed to work miracles, has been venerated since the early sixteenth century. The*

sculptor is unknown but the work is thought to have been made between about 1505 and 1512. It represents the Virgin Mary holding the dead body of Christ on her lap, a type of devotional image known as a Pietà or Vesperbild or, in Spain, Madre Dolorosa. The veneration of this type of image began in Germany and became widespread in Spain from the fifteenth century.

There are documents which show that the cult of the Virgin of the Camino was already well established in 1513, but none which confirm that it was originally related to any image. According to legend, the Virgin appeared miraculously before a shepherd

12

THROUGH GALICIA
León to Compostella

named Alvar Simón and ordered that a hermitage or oratory dedicated to her be built by the roadside near León. This account received papal confirmation in a bull dated 1517. Documents about the sanctuary are scarce. It is known that a church had been 'recently built' in 1513 (on the site of an older building) but there is no record of the date that the sculpture found its way there.

It is tempting to speculate that the new building was erected specifically to house the image and that the story of Alvar Simón's vision is what is called a 'myth of origin'. That is to say, it is a story invented to provide divine sanction for an existing cult. The sculpture can be seen today on the high altar of an impressive modern church founded in 1957. It stands on the site of the original sanctuary about three miles from León, and replaces the church mentioned by Laffi, which was begun in 1645. That one was still unfinished by the time of his visit. See Salvador y Conde, J., La Virgen del Camino, León, 1980.

E The former hospice from which the Hospital de Orbigo gets its name was no longer in existence in Laffi's day. Its site is marked by a cross.

WHEN WE ARRIVED IN LEÓN WE WENT AT once to the bishop to have the dimissory signed. After that we went to the cathedral, which is magnificent and very old,[a] but not like the one at Burgos. In this city there are some truly ancient buildings, because it is the metropolis of the whole kingdom of León and was the former seat of the kings. It is large, with large religious houses of both monks and nuns. It lies in a plain and is ringed by walls. A large river[b] flows past the west side of the town. On the near bank of the river is a very big and rich hospice called St Mark's, with a beautiful church. The monks here give the *passada* to pilgrims. Here too there is a large bridge spanning the river. We went to look for lodgings and next morning went to say Mass in St Isidore. They gave us alms for three masses in addition to the one we had said. After this Mass we walked about the city again, and observed how very beautiful, prosperous and grand it is. A great fair was being held, where there was everything in plenty.[c]

We left the city, passing the hospice with its monks who give the *passada* to pilgrims and also bless their staffs, as they do in Burgos. We went over the large bridge I have mentioned and continued our journey, climbing a hill on which they are building a fine church for a miraculous image which they call the Virgin of the Way.[d]

From there we went to San Miguel del Camino, two leagues away, which is a very small village, all of huts roofed with straw. We continued to Puente de Orbigo, where we spent the night, though miserably, since we had to sleep on the ground. The inhabitants are so poor that they need alms, so you pay them for a shelter they provide in their huts.[e]

In the morning we set out from Puente de Orbigo and after passing through two small villages came to Astorga, three leagues away. This town and its lands are the domain of the Marquis of Astorga. It is a handsome place, situated on a slope, round which are great stretches of cultivated land, partly in the plain and partly on the slope. It is surrounded by high, strong walls, all built of masonry, with frequent round towers at regular intervals. There are three gates, one of which, on the east side, leads into a broad plain where there are a number of religious houses of monks and nuns. It is very narrow, allowing only one man to pass at a time, and I think must serve as a sallyport rather than anything else. The second gate, towards the north, is broad, and outside it are convents and many houses and gardens and other delights. This is the gate by which you enter the town on arrival. The third gate, on the west, is like-

A *Astorga was the capital of the region long before the Roman era. The Romans developed it and it was designated Asturica Augusta by the Emperor Augustus. Parts of the Roman wall are still standing. The walls and gates that Laffi saw were built in the thirteenth century, but were demolished in the nineteenth. Astorga was always an important centre for Compostellan pilgrims and had many hospices. It is here that the pilgrimage road from Salamanca, the Camino de la Plata, joins the Camino Francés. The cathedral, originally Romanesque, was rebuilt beginning in 1471. The facade is Baroque. Among the carvings, admired by Laffi, on the main portal is St James, dressed as a pilgrim, kneeling before Christ.*

B *24 June.*

C *Foncebadón.*

wise broad. This is the gate by which you leave Astorga. On the right hand is the cathedral, which is old and very fine. It is graced with the finest marble statuary and figures. It is well administered by the canons. In front of the door is a fine marble arch. To the right of the cathedral is the bishop's palace, and to the left the hospice, where they are very charitable to pilgrims. There are some splendid houses. The town is very prosperous, with a fine square, which is situated almost at the end of the town on the east side. It is surrounded by arcades and is very accessible.[a]

So we left Astorga and went to Rabanal, five leagues on, going through two or three small villages on the way. Rabanal is situated half way up a hill in a very fertile area. Here we stayed the night, and in the morning which was the feast day of St John the Baptist,[b] we continued up the hill to a small village[c] where we said Mass and were given alms. Then we went on through the hills, passing through several other small villages. Here we were hit by a very violent storm, with wind and rain, which left us almost dead. But it was followed by a very hot sun, which dried our clothes. So we kept going through the hills, until the way began to descend on the west side. We reached Molinaseca, six very long leagues away, which is the first place after these great hills. It is situated in a fair plain, with a river on its east side which flows all year round. It has plenty of fruit and vegetables, rather than grain. Beyond it extends a great, broad plain, in which there are many pleasant villages.

From here we went on to Ponferrada, two leagues away, an excellent place that has plenty of everything. It has a large, attractive square, and many monasteries and fine houses. We stayed the night here and next morning walked around the town. A funeral service was being performed, so we went into the church to observe the local customs. The close relatives of the deceased sit on a special bench while the Office is sung. After the service they go to the door of the church and give alms to the people leaving the

LEÓN TO COMPOSTELLA

———

Fig. 64 A view of the city of Astorga, first third of 17th century, as it appeared to Laffi. It depicts a thanksgiving procession which followed the accidental entombment of some well-diggers who were saved by their inter-cession to the Virgin. The city gate in the background is the former Puerta de Rey through which pilgrims from France entered. Today the approach-road is called the Street of the Well. Painting by Juan de Pena-losa y Sandoval. (Courtesy of Sres D D. Bernardo and Hortensio Velado Grana.)

———

church; and after this they go home, accompanied by all the mourners. They are dressed in black in a long garment like a monk's habit, with a tail and two sleeves which they trail along the ground. They wear a very large hat pulled down over their eyes, with a broad brim that falls down all round, so that you can hardly see who they are. They keep their hands out of sight under their robe. They – that is, only the relatives of the deceased – go three by three. The others accompany them to the door of their house and then leave them.

We stayed to see the whole of this ceremony and then went on to Cacabelos, which lies in the same plain. We passed through many pleasant, fertile places, and came to Villafranca del Bierzo, two leagues away. This is a very agreeable place lying in a valley between four high hills, where two large rivers meet.[a] It is the last village in the kingdom of León, though it would be better called a town because of its size and prosperous air. It has many religious houses of both monks and nuns, a large square and some very splendid houses. There is also a large hospice for pilgrims. In the morning we went to the Jesuit Fathers to say Mass,[b] and they gave us alms and breakfast.

In this large town – I say large, for there are places which are not so large nor so noble as this – they are very charitable to pilgrims, particularly those wearing the heavy cloak that they call the *cappa*. They give this charity without being asked. The reason for this was explained to us by a Franciscan Observantine when we went to see his monastery.[c] We were told that the tradition was known to many people in this place.

They say that a young and devout pilgrim arrived on his way to St James and asked for charity all over the village but found no one who would give it to him, so he became greatly distressed. By chance he passed by an inn (which they call *tenda* or *taverna*) and asked for alms. The innkeeper, seeing that he wore a fine cloak, asked him to come in and said that that is what he would provide. He went in and sat down, and the innkeeper gave him a meal. Then, having eaten, he got up, thinking that he had only to thank his host and continue on his way. But the innkeeper retorted that he must pay for his meal, and contemptuously took his cloak from him. The poor young man went sorrowfully on his way, all the while grieving until he came to

St James of Galicia. After praying at the saint's altar, he climbed up the steps behind the altar to embrace the statue of St James which stands above it, for to embrace it reverently is to receive plenary indulgence. Reaching the top of the steps, he embraced the statue with loving tears and then he noticed that his cloak was round the statue. He shouted for joy at the miracle, and all the other pilgrims who were there and all the canons in the sacristy ran to see him.

On hearing the young man's story, the bishop of Compostella sent men to Villafranca to make inquiries and ascertain what had happened. The innkeeper, when asked if he had a cape to sell, said he had one which he had bought from a pilgrim. He had put it in a chest which he had locked and not since opened. But when he now opened the chest

he was dumbfounded to find that it was not there. The men from Compostella, who stood there looking on, asked him what was the matter and where was the cloak. The inn-keeper made the excuse that it must have been stolen. Then he was arrested by the authorities, confessed everything and was punished as he deserved. The bishop's men re-turned to Compostella and told him what had happened. Realising that this was the truth of the matter, the bishop thanked God and St James for the miracle and sent the young man off with his cloak. So, from that time onwards they have always provided charity for pilgrims, especially those who, as I said, wear a cape or cloak.

After this we went to the Discalced Sisters,[a] where the Germans had also gone to sell their parchment saints, which the Spanish call *vitelas*.[b] Then we left, crossing a large bridge on the west side, and continued beside the river to Herrerías, two leagues away, which is situated on the river bank. Here they excavate iron from the hills and bring it to the village, where there is a furnace for smelting it. They have a large iron hammer which is driven by water

Fig. 65 *The former Puerta de Sol, Astorga, through which pilgrims from the south, on the Camino de la Plata, entered the city. (Courtesy of Sres D D. Bernardo and Hor-tensio Velado Grana.)*

Fig. 66 *Padlock and key (17th century) of the former Puerta de Sol. The gate was closed every day at nightfall. (Courtesy of Sres D D. Ber-nardo and Hortensio Velado Grana.)*

Herrerías means 'ironworks'. It lies in the middle of a busy mining region that has been worked since Roman times. Its industrial centre is Ponferrada ('Iron Bridge'). The bridge at Ponferrada was built by the bishop of Astorga at the end of the eleventh century expressly to help pilgrims. It was constructed of granite reinforced with iron clamps. At Compludo, some twelve miles south of Ponferrada there is a medieval foundry still working today, which is powered by a waterwheel that drives a hammer, much the same as Laffi describes.

power, as well as forging tongs and bellows. All these tools are of immense size. The village is small and nearly all its huts are roofed with straw. It is the first place you come to in the kingdom of Galicia. At the top of a hill there is a castle that marks the frontier and guards the mouth of the river where you enter Galicia.[a]

At this point you leave the river and begin to climb a great mountain called Monte Cebrero. We spent the night at the bottom, sleeping in the open air, and in the morning we began our ascent. We came to La Faba, a village half way up the mountain, a distance of four leagues, and continued to climb to the top. There is a Benedictine monastery here, where the monks give pilgrims a *passada* of bread, wine and other alms. There is also a hospice for pilgrims.

They have here a celebrated holy relic consisting of a

consecrated wafer converted into the true body of Christ our Lord and a glass phial containing wine which was converted into his true blood. It came about this way. At the summit of the mountain, before the present monastery was built, there lived a hermit who was French and was doing penance. He was a monk and said Mass every morning. The people of La Faba, the village half way up the mountain, came to hear Mass whenever they could. Among them was a peasant who never failed to come even in the rain, the snow or other bad weather. It happened that one morning, when it had been snowing heavily, the man, on hearing the hermit's bell, set out to struggle to the top through the deep snow that lay on the road. Finally, with much effort, he got to the top and reached the church. But by this time the monk had already performed the Elevation of the Host and

Fig. 67 *Medieval pilgrim's bridge at Molinaseca, now little used.*

Fig. 68 *The figure of St Francis of Assisi above the west door of the Franciscan church, Villafranca.*

LEÓN TO COMPOSTELLA

The Benedictine abbey of el Cebrero was said to have been founded in 836 though the oldest documents that mention it date from the end of the eleventh century. It was closed in the nineteenth century and only the church remains. It contains the greatly venerated relics, kept in silver caskets, as well as the chalice and paten, of the event described by Laffi. It is said to have occurred about 1300 and is recorded in a papal bull and other early documents. (The peasant came not from La Faba but from Barjamayor nearby.) The church also contains two tombs which, according to popular belief, hold the remains of the monk and the peasant. An image of the 'Virgin of the Miracle' stands above the altar. Her head is inclined, the result, it is said, of having nodded at the sight of it. Claims have been made that the chalice is the original Holy Grail, though the workmanship appears to be twelfth century.

———

Fig. 69 *Part of the mechanism (water-wheel and cam-shaft) that activates the hammer in the foundry at Compludo. The present building is probably not earlier than 15th century, though tradition puts its foundation in the 7th century.*

———

was about to give communion. The peasant entered the church, very upset at not arriving in time for the whole of the Mass, and began to beat the snow off his cloak and boots. The hermit, who was at that moment holding the wafer ready for communion, heard the man making a lot of noise beating his feet and cloak. He turned round to look at him, saying to himself: 'Just look at this poor man who has come here this morning through such thick snow, at the risk of his life, just to hear Mass and see the lifting up of a wafer which, after all, is nothing more than a piece of bread!' Hardly had he uttered these impious words than he saw the consecrated wafer turning into real, actual flesh, the size of a finger – which I have seen with my own eyes – and the wine similarly turning into real blood of our Lord, congealed into a single piece. The blood is still preserved in a glass phial and the wafer in a crystal chalice, kept in the tabernacle together with the Host. Pope Paschal 11 wished to see this miracle when he went to St James of Galicia dressed as a pilgrim, as I shall explain in my account of Compostella. Apart from the fact that I have seen it with my own eyes, we know about these things from the records of many authors.[a]

After seeing the holy relic we went on our way through the mountains, passing through a number of small villages inhabited by shepherds. Then we began to descend. After a long walk we came at last into a plain, where there was a village of some size, with good houses, called Triacastela, six leagues away. Here, one of the Germans who was travelling with us went down with a fever, so his companions looked for a horse to take him to the nearest village to be treated. We bade them goodbye and continued on our journey, climbing steeply and passing through many hills until we began to descend towards a small village, a distance of two leagues. We passed through this village, still going downhill, until we came to a pleasant, fertile plain, growing plenty of fruit of all kinds. There were many houses, orchards and gardens. Then we crossed a river where there are several mills, and climbed the road to Sarriá two leagues away. This is a very fine, prosperous town, with attractive houses and a monastery of the white friars who give pilgrims a *passada*. Above the town is a splendid, strong castle surrounded by very high walls, where the lord of the town lives. He also gives a *passada*, in the form of money, to

A *At the time of Laffi's visit the monastery (called the Convent of the Magdalene) was administered by the Order of Mercedarians, as it is still today. Their main concerns were tending the sick and rescuing Christians who had been taken prisoner by the Moors. To this end they even offered their own person as hostages.*

pilgrims coming from Compostella, and acts as magistrate, being absolute ruler hereabouts.[a]

After we left Sarriá we had another long climb into the hills called the Montes de Sarriá and then arrived at Puertomarin, a distance of three leagues. This is a fine town. Through the middle flows a large river with plenty of fish, particularly eels and excellent trout, which provided us with a magnificent supper. Along the river are large vineyards and many orchards. One half of the town lies on the near side of the river, the other half on the far side, the two

Fig. 70 *Fortified priory church (12th century) of San Juan, patron of the Hospitallers, at Puertomarin. It is one of the buildings dismantled in the valley bottom and rebuilt on the hillside.*

The town, as Laffi describes it, no longer exists. It once lay at the bottom of a steep-sided valley, through which the River Miño runs, but in 1963 a dam was built so that it became submerged. A new town was built on the hillside to which major monuments were transported stone by stone before the waters rose. The pilgrim's hospice was demolished.

C *The spring was at a place called Lavacolla, where pilgrims performed what was, in effect, a rite of purification by washing. It was a symbolic cleansing before entering the sacred precincts of the city. The original meaning of the place-name (called Lavamentula in the* Pilgrim's Guide*) seems to be 'a washing of one's private parts' though it was apparently usual to wash the whole body. See Shaver-Crandell, A., Gerson, P., Stones, A.,* The Pilgrim's Guide to Santiago de Compostela, *London, 1995; and Hohler, C., 'A Note on* Jacobus', Warburg Institute Journal, *vol. 35 (1972), pp. 31-80.*

Monte del Gozo, or Mountjoy in English, originally denoted the stone cairns that were erected by the wayside to guide travellers. For French pilgrims it became a popular cry, 'Montjoie!', shouted on first setting eyes on their journey's end. It is said that Charlemagne uttered it on first seeing Rome from the top of Monte Mario. He then dismounted and entered the city barefoot, like a penitent.

parts being connected by a large, splendid bridge, which gives the place its name, Puente del Miño.[b]

Next morning, having said Mass, we went to Ligonde, a small village four long leagues away, and Mellid, another six. Here we spent some time looking around the town, which is attractive but not very big. It has a fine monastery of the Franciscan Observantines as well as a number of houses. Next morning we were on our way to a place called Ferreiros, two leagues, and Amenal, a small and impoverished village three short leagues further on. From there we continued until we came to a spring, where we thoroughly refreshed ourselves and changed our clothes, for we knew we were near St James. From this spring we climbed for about half a league to the top of a hill called the Monte del Gozo. From here we could discern Santiago, the city we had so much longed to reach, some half a league away.[c]

On seeing the city we fell to our knees and, with tears of great joy falling from our eyes, we began to sing the 'Te Deum'. But we had sung no more than two or three verses when we found ourselves unable to utter the words because of the copious tears which streamed from our eyes, so intense were our feelings. Our hearts were full and our unceasing tears made us give up singing, until finally, having unburdened ourselves and spent our tears, we resumed singing the 'Te Deum'. Singing as we walked, we carried on down to the outer suburbs of Compostella, a large, splendid district, which is all the while being built upon. We passed through and came to the gate of the town.

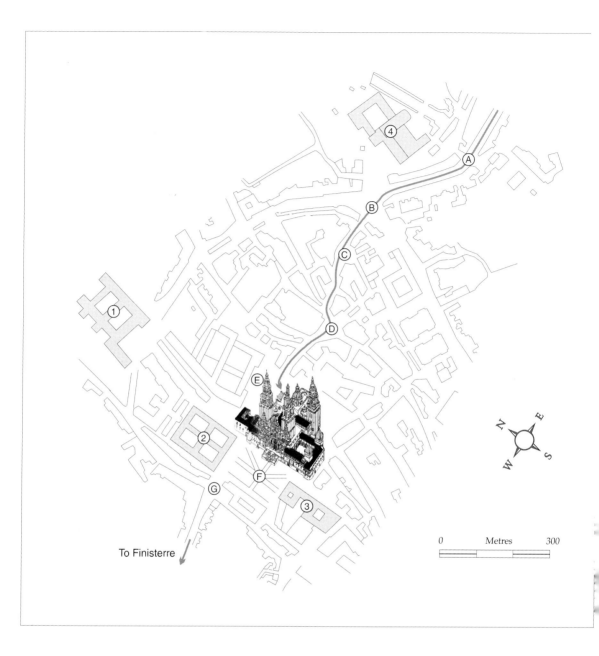

Fig. 71 *Santiago
de Compostela, with the
route followed by Laffi
when arriving.*

1 *Franciscan Monastery*
2 *Hostal de los Reyes Católicos*
3 *College of San Jerome*
4 *Iglesia de Santo Domingo*

A *Rúa de San Pedro*
B *Puerta del Camino*
C *Calle de las Casas Reales*
D *Plaza de Cervantes*
E *Puerta del Paraíso*
F *Plaza del Obradoiro*
G *Puerta de las Huertas*

13

THE BOURN &

AN UNEXPECTED MEETING

Santiago de Compostela

A *Laffi made his way to the cathedral along the route traditionally taken by pilgrims. From the city gate, the Puerta del Camino (no longer standing), he followed a narrow street, the Calle de las Casas Reales, to reach the Plaza de Cervantes, then a busy market-place. From here the way took him to a square outside the north door of the cathedral. The door is known as the Gate of Paradise, the Puerta del Paraíso. The present north façade is Baroque and was begun in 1762, replacing the earlier Romanesque front which Laffi would have seen. The square and the façade are called the Azabacheria, or 'carvers of jet', and recall the medieval booths and stalls that once stood there selling such wares, together with everyday necessities for pilgrims. The monastery of Santo Domingo was founded in 1220, following a second visit to the city by St Dominic when he established a community of friars.*

WE ENTERED THROUGH A GATE BUILT ENtirely of masonry. In front of it is a fine bridge, also of stone. A little stream runs under it, going along the east side of the city wall towards the south. Outside the gate is the splendid monastery of Santo Domingo and many other fine buildings. Once inside we followed a street leading directly to a square, which is not very big and is triangular in shape. Here they have all kinds of fruit in plenty, as well as other necessities, and all quite cheap. The bread and wine are particularly good. We left the market place by the west corner and came to the side door of the church of St James. In front of it is an attractive square, which you enter by way of a flight of steps. They are made of the same flagstones as the paving of the square itself.[a]

We went through the door, which is of splendid workmanship, all of marble, and approached the high altar of St James. There we knelt, in great joy and with a contrite heart, for never before had we experienced any such thing. We thanked God and the apostle for having led us safe and sound to the goal we had so longed for, after a journey of such length, with all its toil and anxieties. Then we went behind the altar and climbed a few steps, where we could embrace the apostle's image.

This is a life-size statue. If you kiss it reverently you will be granted plenary indulgence, though you are not allowed to touch the sacred body itself. Pilgrims put their cape on the statue and their hat on its head while they embrace it, and then stay a few moments. After making this devotion we descended on the other side and once more prayed before the saint's altar. Then we walked round the church, marvelling greatly at everything.

The building is in the form of a cross. In the upper part of

A *In the crypt.*

B *In the ambulatory.*

C *25 July.*

D *The chapel is formally dedicated to the 'Holy Saviour' and is part of the Romanesque church that was begun in 1075. It later became known as the chapel of the King of France following an endowment made by the French king, Charles V (1337-80). King Louis IX (1214-70) made the pilgrimage to Compostella. He was a man of great piety and also an active crusader and was canonised in 1297. Pilgrim's certificates, known as 'Compostelas' are still issued, but only to those who have travelled on foot or on bicycle.*

E *East.*

F *North and south.*

G *Laffi makes a strange mistake about the orientation of the cathedral (which I have corrected where necessary). The west door according to him faces south, the other facades being given correspondingly wrong bearings. Marble is used much less in the building than he suggests. The principal material is a Galician stone, 'Coimbra' granite, which is softer and more workable than other types of granite. The south door only has marble jambs. The doors are no longer of bronze.*

H *The appearance of churches and other public buildings throughout the city underwent a complete transformation which began in the early 16th century (following the final expulsion of the Moors from*

the cross, that is to say, in the place where you would find the panel inscribed INRI, there stands the high altar. Beneath it[a] rests the body of the glorious apostle, St James. Above the altar is a magnificent, gilded baldachin, with sculptures in the round. It was begun in 1666 and finished in 1673. Around the altar at the back,[b] is a series of black marble columns [that form the jambs] of a series of chapels encircling the altar. Among these chapels is a very remarkable one, dedicated to the king of France, where they issue certificates to pilgrims (which you have to pay for). This chapel, built when St Louis, king of France, went to Santiago, lies directly behind the saint's altar. To the right of the chapel is the Holy Door, which they open in Holy Year, that is to say, whenever the feast of St James[c] falls on a Sunday. This is done nowhere else except here and at Rome.[d]

If you follow the series of columns and chapels round the whole church, which, as I said, is in the form of a cross, you will come to a door at the end of each arm of the cross. Thus there are four doors: the one at the top of the cross, which is the Holy Door,[e] the doors in the two lateral arms,[f] and the

164   SANTIAGO DE COMPOSTELA

Spain in 1492) and lasted until the second half of the 18th century. Medieval buildings, mainly Romanesque and Gothic, were gradually converted (that is to say, often reclad rather than rebuilt) in Baroque thanks to the deliberate policies of a succession of clergy who were knowledgeable and enthusiastic about contemporary European architecture. Laffi's visits (between 1666 and 1673) took place at a time when these developments were gathering pace.

Of the four towers that Laffi mentions only one was a bell-tower. This is the south tower of the pair that flank the west facade. Its renovation was completed in 1669-70. Its pair, called the Carraca Tower, was somewhat later, 1687. (Their pinnacles, the finishing touches, were added in 1720-32.) Of the other two, the one at the end of the south transept is the Clock Tower (1676-80). The other has disappeared.

great door which faces west. They are magnificent doors, all worked in bronze and framed in the finest marble, as is used for the rest of the church.[g]

There are four bell-towers, three of which were being built while we were there. The first to be finished will be 90 *braccia* high and have ten bells. They look very fine. There is one tower on each side of the main facade of the church, the other two being on each side of the head of the cross. The facade that faces west is, indeed, magnificent, and the whole elevation is well-designed architecturally. Then there is decorative interlacing in the Spanish style. Above it are balustrades along which you can walk. Over the west door is a very fine Last Judgement, the figures carved in *mezzo-rilievo.*[h]

The famous Baroque west front, the Obradoiro, did not exist in Laffi's time. It was added between 1738 and 1750 and, from the outside, completely hides the older Romanesque-Gothic facade that he so admired. The Last Judgement on the Portal of Glory was carved by a master-sculptor who is known only as Mateo and was finished in 1188. (The date and sculptor's name are on the underside of the lintel.) Behind the central pillar, at its foot, is a small kneeling figure, thought to be Mateo.

Fig. 74 *Drawing of*
the west front of the cathedral
before the addition of the
Baroque facade, by José de Vega
y Verdugo, c. 1655-7, from his
Memoria sobre las Obras en la
Catedral de Santiago. *(Archivo*
de la Catedral de Compostela;
Photo: Xenaro
Martinez Castro.)

Outside the west door is a beautiful and very unusual stairway.[a] It has a double flight, one on each side, and at the top it is separated from the church by a terrace. You go down it into a great square,[b] graced with some splendid buildings, particularly on the north side. Here there is a fine hospital that can hold a thousand sick people. The beds are arranged in the form of a cross so that everyone can hear Mass from a chapel which stands by itself in the centre. There are three lovely courtyards all built of marble[c] each one exhibiting a different classical order, one Corinthian, another Doric and the third, Tuscan. Each has a spacious yard with a single fountain in the centre. They are charming, being decorated in a variety of different styles. It is well worth seeing, not so much for its age as for its beauty. The

SANTIAGO DE COMPOSTELA

Fig. 75 *Part of the relief of the Last Judgement (1188) above the west doors of Compostella cathedral. Six of the twenty-four 'Elders of the Apocalypse', with psaltery, organistrum and viols.*

———

A *It dates from c. 1603-6.*

B *Plaza del Obradoiro.*

C *Granite, mainly.*

D *The Hostal, or Hospital, de los Reyes Católicos was founded expressly for pilgrims at the beginning of the 16th century by the 'Catholic Monarchs', Isabel and Fernando (not Alfonso). Their reign saw the final defeat of the Moors in Spain and laid the foundations of future Spanish*

exterior of the hospital, just as much as the interior, is like a royal palace. It was the king, Don Alfonso, who had it built.[d]

After leaving here, we found an inn where we settled in for the rest of our stay at Compostella. Early next morning we went to St James's to celebrate Mass, and then went to look for the person in charge of the building works at the cathedral. He was a nobleman of the city and a canon, with the title of Cardinal of the church of St James. We gave him some rather unusual things we had brought from Italy, which I had promised him the first time I came to Compostella. They were some very good drawings by our best artists, which he dearly wanted. He invited us to stay and dine

power. The hospital was a new building, not an old one renovated, and the sovereigns involved themselves closely in its design and construction. Laffi's figure of one thousand beds is not to taken literally, though it is recorded that 2588 sick persons were treated between 1539 and 1541.

When it was opened the hospital provided accommodation for the healthy as well as the sick, but this amenity was eventually withdrawn for lack of money.

The original building had only two courtyards, those at the front that today occupy the south-west and south-east quarters. In Laffi's

*time a third had been added be-
hind them that occupied the
whole width of the building. This
was converted into two in the
mid-18th century, to give the plan
that we see today. The original
style was Plateresque, still to be
seen on the central doorway overlooking the square. Additions
were made up to the 18th century,
including a remarkable Baroque
staircase. In 1954 the building was
turned into an hotel.*

*A contemporary of Laffi ob-
served: 'I believe that this hospital
is so well known in every part of
the world that all I can say about
it will be readily credited. In the
three large wards there are few
days when there are fewer than
two hundred sick people, and the
number is much larger in jubilee
year. Yet every patient is treated
with as much care as if the hospital had been erected for his particular benefit. The hospital is one
of the great things of the earth.
Apart from its sumptuousness and
the regal grandeur of its architecture it is a marvellous thing to feel
its size, the multitude of its staff,
the diligence and zeal of the attendants, the cleanliness of the
linen, the care taken about the
cooking, the perfect order of the
routine and the assiduity of the
doctors. One may indeed regard it
as the crowning glory of Christendom' (Molina, Luis de,* Descrip-
ción del Reino de Galicia,
1675).

A *The canon in charge of building
works was José de Vega y Verdugo,
Count of Alba Real, who took up
his post in 1658. He was a key figure in the Baroque development
of the cathedral, his influence being felt long after his departure*

with him and served us a sumptuous banquet. Afterwards
he gave us many presents.[a]

As he was in charge of the works at St James's, this gentleman took us round the whole church. We saw some fine
things that in the ordinary way are not so easily seen by pilgrims. First, we went all round the outside of the building
and then up on the roof. It is all covered with white marble,
as it were like a flight of steps, rising so that you can reach
all the upper part of the church. Round the roof, on the
outside, is a beautiful balustrade with statues and various
other sculptures. To stand on the roof of the church was
rather like being in a beautiful garden. The dome, which is

situated on the roof immediately above the high altar, has
a marble[b] cross done in the form of a lily and all fretted.
There is a wide opening in the dome, through which pilgrims may pass, but, so it is commonly said, those who are
in mortal sin find they cannot do so. But that, so the canon
told us, is a mere superstition of ignorant people.

We went up inside the bell-towers, which are very
strongly built, with an inner wall like a fortress. In the oldest bell-tower, which stands on the south we saw the bell
that rang when the miracle took place of the pilgrim who
was wrongly hanged at Santo Domingo de la Calzada,

*Fig. 76   The Obradoiro,
the west front of Compostella
cathedral, 1738-50.*

*Fig. 77   The stepped roof
over the nave of Compostella
cathedral, looking west, with
the figure of St James.*

which I described earlier. There was also the bell that rang of its own accord when St Louis, king of France, arrived at Compostella. They sawed off half of one side in memory of that occasion, so that it could never be rung again. Many ignorant folk tell ridiculous stories about the bell. In particular they say that, when the king of Spain learned that the king of France had been to Compostella and that, on his arrival in the church, the great bell had rung of its own accord, he said to himself, 'If this bell has rung of its own accord for the king of France, who is a foreigner, then if I, who am their Sire, go there, not only will this bell ring, but

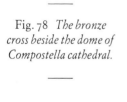

Fig. 78 *The bronze cross beside the dome of Compostella cathedral.*

SANTIAGO DE COMPOSTELA

A *Laffi distinguishes between two bell-towers. This is hard to follow for there was, and is, only one. The first cannot refer to the clock tower because it was not built until after his last visit to Compostella. The 'great bell-tower' is properly described. The central 'donjon', round which the stairs rise, is rectangular. The thick outer wall has openings in which the bells hang. Today there are fourteen.*

The pitched roof does indeed resemble a huge staircase, being built of rows of fairly thick, rectangular slabs of granite (not marble), each row overlapping the one below. The granite was once covered with conventional quarry tiles, which have since been removed.

B *The pallium was once sent to individual prelates as a mark of special honour, but was later more widely granted, occasionally to bishops as well as archbishops. It symbolizes the 'plenitude of the pontifical office'. It is woven from wool blessed on St Agnes's day in the church of St Agnes fuori le Mura at Rome.*

C *No longer done.*

all the bells in the kingdom of Galicia.' They say that he did go, and that not only did the bells of Galicia remain silent, but even that one which had rung for the king of France. Then the Spanish people, and even the king himself, on seeing this, took it as an insult. They had the bell sawn through, breaking it so that it could no longer ring for anyone, because it had rung for a foreigner, but not for their own king. And so they broke it. But this, as I said, is all idle talk of ignorant people.

Next we went into the great bell-tower where there are twelve bells. It is truly well worth seeing, and is just like a palace. The bell-ringer, who occupies it, wanted to provide drinks for us, and for all the canon's attendants as well. The bells are hung all round the tower, at the windows in the walls. The wall is double, the inner one forming, as I said, a kind of donjon.[a]

We then went down into the church and waited awhile, until they came to celebrate High Mass. I truly believe there is no other church, except St Peter's at Rome, where they organize it so well as they do here. First the archbishop entered, wearing full pontificals, including the pallium, as is worn by the Pope himself. Apart from the Pope, the pallium may be worn by no one else except the archbishop of Compostella. This dignity was conferred on him by Paschal 11 in 1104. Behind the archbishop who, as I said, was in pontificals with mitre and pastoral staff, came the canons. They are known here by the courtesy title of cardinal, a dignity also conferred by the Pope. They too were wearing pontificals with a bishop's mitre. There were nine canons, all dressed the same way.[b]

When the solemn feast of High Mass has been celebrated by the archbishop, the canons then take turns to officiate, day by day. They stand beneath the baldachin, arrayed in their vestments, which are in every way different from the archbishop's, each one taking his turn throughout the week until they reach the beginning again.[c] One cannot speak too highly of the grace and solemnity they habitually bring to performing the Offices in this church.

Before the high altar is a great thurible in the shape of a large lamp, attached by a rope to the ceiling at the very top of the dome. It is lowered when they put in the incense and light it. Then they draw it to one side, to such a height that only a few can still reach it, and then they give it a push. It

The famous censer, the bota-
fumeiro, *was one of the many
benefactions made to the cathedral by the French king, Louis XI
(1423-83). The original, made of
silver, was snatched by Napoleon.
The present censer, of silver-
plated brass, dates from 1851. In
1483, the year of his death, the
king sent bell-founders, materials
and money for the construction of
two bells, which were to be 'the
biggest that exist in the service of
the church. And there must be
none larger.'*

B *Made of bronze, 1578-84.*

C *The mother of John the Baptist.*

D *Many kinds of bagpipes have been
developed in the different countries of Europe since the Middle
Ages, though the instrument is of
much greater antiquity. There is
evidence of their use as an accom-
paniment to chanting in medieval
monasteries and other religious
houses. Laffi describes the ones he
heard as a* zampogna *and* pive
sordine. *The former is also called
the Calabrian bagpipe. The* pive
*would very likely have been the
Spanish* gaita, *a very popular instrument, though mainly confined
to Galicia. The type of frame-
drum he describes was typically
Spanish. It was square and small
enough to hang from the player's
neck and lie on his chest. He beat
it with his fists, usually clenched.*

E *2 July, since moved.*

swings from one door to the other, that is, from south to
north, along the arms of the cross. Because of its size and
speed it makes a great wind. The burning incense and other
odours produce a thick, fragrant smoke, which permeates
the whole church.[a]

In front of the altar is an iron grille that is always kept
closed while Mass is being sung. On the left side of the grille
is a pulpit, where the sub-deacon ascends to read the epistle
to the congregation. Similarly, on the right is another pulpit, from which the deacon reads the gospel.[b] When Mass
was over – which, as I said, was sung – we went to have dinner. Afterwards, we rested for a while to pass the midday
hours. Then suddenly we heard the bell being rung for Vespers so we returned to St James's. A procession was just beginning for the feast of St Elizabeth.[c] I shall describe it to
you, because it was very different from the way we celebrate
it. First came many drummers, each one accompanied by a
player who had one or other of two kinds of bagpipes, and
another instrument rather like a window-frame with parchment stretched across both sides. It is played the way we
play the tambourine in Italy, but it makes a great noise.
They went two by two, each pair with a drummer. It took
three people to play the big drum, including two who carry
it on a litter, to which two staves are attached. The bearers
go side by side, while the drummer stands behind, just as
he would with a big drum.[d]

After the players came a succession of young people in
various groups, all wearing masks. They danced in procession, in sets of four, and played castanets. Next came the
effigy of whichever saint they might be celebrating that day.
On this occasion the saints were the Blessed Virgin and
St Elizabeth, as it was the feast of the Visitation.[e] They carried the statues under a big, beautiful decorated baldachin,
and brought many thuribles for censing. It is quite apparent how much reverence they feel, since it is all done with
so much solemnity. Behind the baldachin came men and
then women. When the procession was over they put the
statues of the Blessed Virgin and St Elizabeth on the altar.
Then, after many prayers and censing, they formed themselves into a great circle and began to play all their instruments. The young men, all wearing their masks, dance with
one another and play their pipes. The young women group
themselves opposite, with cymbals and castanets. All this

Fig. 79 *The Bota-fumeiro censer.*

F *A celebration of this kind carries strong echoes of much older rites of pagan origin. Folk-dance and folk-song, intended to invoke the nature gods, were among the most deeply ingrained habits of rural communities and the wearing of masks was a feature of some festivals. There is much evidence to show that among people newly converted to Christianity such activities found their way into churches. What the clergy were unable to prevent they adapted to Christian worship. Guidelines had been laid down in the 6th century: 'Take care not to destroy the temples of idols. They must pass from the cult of demons to the service of the true God. So long as people see that these ancient places of devotion remain standing they will be more disposed to betake themselves there from the tendency of habit' (Gregory the Great, in a letter to Augustine of Canterbury, missionary to England in 597:* Patrologia Latina, *vol.* LXXVII, *lib. xii, Epist. 76, cols. 1215-16).*

while they were singing psalms and praying out loud, as seemed only proper. The church itself might have collapsed, so great was the din, in particular from the drums and bagpipes, and also bells.*f*

When this festive occasion was over we went back to the inn as it was now evening. Next morning we went back to St James's to say Mass. While there I heard my companion's

173

A The Franciscan monastery that
Laffi saw was a Gothic building,
of which there now remains only
five arches on the north side of the
main cloister. Reconstruction in
the Baroque style began in the late
17th century. The monastery was
the first Franciscan foundation in
the Iberian peninsula. It was
founded, according to tradition,
by St Francis himself who is said
to have made the pilgrimage to
Compostella in 1214. The city
formerly had nine gates. Only one
is still standing, the Puerta de
Mazarelos, to the south-east near
the university.

B The Obradoiro.

C Puerta de las Huertas, on the pilgrimage road to Finisterre.

confession and gave him communion. Our devotions done, we went for a walk through the city, which is not very big. It has four gates and two suburbs outside the walls, one outside the east gate, as I mentioned, the other outside the west. The city is situated on a hill and slopes down towards the south. The surrounding walls are all of masonry. Outside the north-west gate is a splendid, very old monastery of the Observantine Franciscans. The buildings are worth seeing, both because of their age and, so we were told, because they were founded by St Francis himself. Their church possesses many treasures.[a]

The gate at the west of the city is remarkable, because there is a great square in front of it,[b] all paved, which faces the main facade of the cathedral. To one side is the facade of the hospital, on the other is a palace that is just as splendid. All the buildings are of stone-work – you will not find any brickwork here, such as we use in Italy. As you go out through this gate,[c] there are two descending flights of stone steps, one beside the other. They are very striking to look at. No beasts of any sort can get through this gate, because

Fig. 80 The gaita, a Spanish bagpipe. From Las Cantigas de Alfonso X (c. 1280), in the monastery of the Escorial, Madrid (MS B I 2). It is Cantiga no. 350 from the third of the MSS produced for the king and the most complete as to numbers (c. 430) and musical iconography. (Courtesy of Professor D. Carlos Villanueva.)

The 'palace' on the south side of the square is the College of St Jerome, formerly a university college, which now houses the rector and administration. It was built in 1556, though its most impressive feature is the great portal that dates from the end of the 15th century. The portal originally formed part of an old pilgrims' hospital that stood in the Plaza de la Azabacheria. It was moved to its present position after the hospital was pulled down in 1651.

of the steps going up and down. Beyond this gate there are many market gardens and orchards watered by springs, so that fruit is plentiful. But it goes rotten quickly, because the air and, indeed, the water itself, is tainted. Yet it looks pure and very clear, so that one is tempted to drink it. Where the water runs it makes the stones turn black, and the whole river bed is the same.[d]

The city once used to be known as Flaúto Brigantio, but is now called Compostella because, when St James's body was brought here it was accompanied by, indeed was guided

Fig. 81 *A frame-drum (13th century), from the collegiate church of Sta Maria de Toro. (Courtesy of Professor D. Carlos Villanueva.)*

A Laffi is wrong about the city's former name, but I have not been able
to trace the source of his error. Bri-
gantium was the ancient name of
La Coruña. The name Compostella appears to have been derived
from the Latin word for a burial
and hence 'a small cemetery'. It
has no connection with medieval
legends concerning a star. It is first
used in documents dating from
1056. A Roman burial ground,
which came to be used as a Christian martyrium from the second
or third century, is known to have
existed under part of the cathedral
and the Plaza de la Quintana.

   Stones, shells and even bones
were sometimes used for inlay,
though the examples Laffi mentions no longer exist.

by, a star. That is why it is known as Compostella, that is to
say, *compos* and *stella*. The city's coat of arms has the star together with a pilgrim's cloak and two crossed staves below.
There are some splendid palaces all built of stone, and all
the squares are paved in the same material. It makes a
splendid sight. Inside the entrances to these palaces, and
likewise on their stairs, the paving is done in inlay, with
very small stones of variegated colours, alternating with
pigs' bones. They use the joints of its feet in particular.
They make a great variety of designs, which look good and
are very durable.[a]

   Having seen the many sights in which this city is so rich,
and seen how well supplied it is with all human necessities,
we returned to St James's, where they were singing High
Mass. We stayed for some time to watch the service, with all
its ritual, and to observe the great crowds who were gathered here from all parts of the world. We wondered whether
there might be anyone from our country. Though we kept
looking we could see no one who, either from their dress or
manner, seemed to be Italian. While we were standing
there, talking together, we were addressed by a man who,
we could tell from his bearing, was well-born. He had a long
red beard and long hair of the same colour, and was dressed
in the English fashion, with a sword at his belt. He asked us
in Latin what country we were from. When we told him we
were Italians from Bologna, he seemed greatly astonished,
saying he could hardly believe it. So we showed him our
citizenship papers, which he read with great interest.

   'My dear fellow-countrymen,' he exclaimed, 'it gives me
the greatest pleasure to have met you here.' He uttered the
words with such ostentatious joy, that at first we suspected
he was lying and merely wanted to relieve us of our money,
for we had heard tell of cases of this kind. So we began to
question him as to the why and wherefore of his leaving
Bologna, and where he was now lodging. But he replied
that, first of all, he wished us to dine with him, when he
would tell us everything. This only aroused our suspicions
still more. However, we were reassured to think that there
were two of us whereas he was alone. We accepted his in-
vitation, so as to find out where he lived. We then accompanied him out of the church, all the while alert to our own
best interests.

   Once outside the church door, it was he who began

B *Count Ercole Zani (1634-84) was a Bolognese nobleman and man of letters. He was a gifted linguist, scientist and mathematician and, later, became a warm anglophile. He travelled widely in Europe, the Near East and Russia. In England he was welcomed by the Royal Society and was received by the king, Charles II. He accompanied the British fleet on an expedition to Tangier before returning to Italy in 1670 by way of Portugal and Spain.*

questioning us, asking for news of Bologna, how such and such a nobleman was faring, or such and such a lady. From certain things that he asked we were bound to conclude that he really was from Bologna. Moreover, his manner of speech and his noble bearing gradually allayed our suspicions, so we now began to congratulate ourselves on having met him. Nevertheless, we were still a little anxious, not knowing who he was. In Bologna we used to know him just by sight because he dressed so bizarrely. Even so, we were now not able to recognize him at all because of that beard, which covered almost the whole of his face.

Discussing this between ourselves, we finally reached the inn where he was staying. We went to his room and sat down, while he went to call the landlord to order a meal. While he was gone we glanced round and saw a little table on which a few letters were lying. Regardless of our bad manners, but determined to satisfy our curiosity, we looked at the addresses on the letters. They read, 'To the most noble and highly esteemed lord, Signore Ercole Zani.'

So, we realized who he was. When he came back to the room we apologized and begged his pardon for not having known him immediately and for having, instead, taken him for some rogue or other. But he only laughed, saying he realized this, and had decided not to tell us sooner who he was, in order to keep us in suspense for a little while. Meanwhile, the meal arrived, which we ate with good cheer, laughing about the incident and giving him much news about Bologna.[b]

When we had eaten we went back to the church together, glad to have met one another. We stayed for Vespers and when that was over we were shown round the treasury by the head of the building works. This treasury contains many valuable pieces: chalices of pure gold, a great quantity of silverware, precious stones, items of jewellery for the altar and, best of all, a bishop's mitre all spangled with pearls and other precious gems. There is much jewellery. There is also a doubloon, or perhaps it would be better called a medallion, which was the first to be struck in Peru, when that country was discovered and conquered by the Spanish. It has the arms of the king of Spain on one side and those of Peru on the other. It weighs twenty-seven pounds, troy weight, and every Spanish pound is sixteen ounces. We also saw many ensigns, standards, tents and

A The naval battle against the Turk-
ish fleet was fought off the town of
Lepanto (Naupaktos) in the Gulf
of Corinth. The crushing defeat of
the Turks by the Christian forces
put an end to what had been an in-
creasingly aggressive threat from
Islam to Christianity in eastern
Europe. The warships of Spain,
Venice, Genoa and the papal states
took part. They were led by Don
John of Austria who represented
Spain. His personal standard, the
Gallardete de Lepanto, is pre-
served in the cathedral museum.
It is eighteen metres long.

B The lantern no longer exists.

other military items. For instance, there is a variety of
weapons, suits of armour and other accoutrements of great
value and renown. They were all things won by Don John of
Austria, commander of the fleet in the great naval battle
against the Turks on 7 October, 1571. This was during the
pontificate of Pius v, now beatified. After the war, Don
John presented to St James's cathedral his commander's
personal standard, which had been given to him by this beatified Pope. The reason was that St James is patron saint
and protector of the whole of Spain.[a]

He also presented many other things of much value that
had been captured from the Turks in the great battle.
Among the many standards belonging to the pashas and
other nobles is the one that belonged to the Sultan's com-
mander-in-chief. There are many carpets and tents, and
also the ship's lantern from the royal galley itself that belonged to the sultan. It is truly something of great price and
remarkable splendour.

On St James's day they bring the lantern out of the treasury, together with all the other things I have mentioned
above. Having lighted it, they place it before the altar of
the holy apostle, where it stays lit for the whole of the High
Mass.[b] The standards likewise they hang up before the
saint, which is something really worth seeing. The treasury
also possesses a large, very long horn from one of the wild
bulls that brought the body of St James from Iria Flavia to
Compostella.

As we had now seen everything we returned to the inn
where Sig. Ercole Zani was lodging and stopped there
gladly, having decided to leave the next day. Before we re-
tired to bed he told us about his journey; how, on leaving
Bologna he had gone to Paris and from there to England.
He left London, the capital of that kingdom, in the company of an ambassador whom the king of England was
sending to Tafilet. They sailed round Spain from north to
west and then south until they reached Tangier – a city of
the kingdom of Morocco, through the straits of Gibraltar.
At Tafilet they were told that the ambassador would not be
received because he was not a true nor good ambassador,
since his king was not true nor good king. So they returned
by way of the western ocean, disembarking at Lisbon, capital of the kingdom of Portugal. Here, Sig. Ercole left his
companion and came on alone to St James in Galicia, in

order to visit the sacred remains and perhaps meet some Italians – as indeed he did.

In the morning we went to St James's to say Mass and afterwards we obtained the certificates that are called 'Compostelas'. Then, having made our devotions, we went to see the great reliquary chapel of St James. Here there lie many sacred relics, some of them very remarkable. There is the cross of the saint himself, also the staff that he carried on his travels through the world. They are in a bronze column attached to the choir screen, on the right, opposite the high altar. After looking at the relics, which are shown to all pilgrims, we were granted our indulgence at the altar of St James. Then we went for a short walk round the city wall in the company of one of the musicians from the cathedral, who was a Roman. He told us the story of a certain Pope,[c] who came to St James's incognito. While he stood at the saint's altar celebrating Mass, there was another priest in the sacristy who, having vested himself, was looking in his missal to see which Mass was to be said on that day. It happened to be the Mass of an apostle. On turning over the page of his missal he observed that the Introit of every Mass began, 'Ecce sacerdos magnus,' – behold the high priest. From this, he realized that the one who at that moment was celebrating Mass at the high altar was, indeed, the high priest himself, that is to say, the Pope. The latter, when he had finished, returned to the sacristy. The priest then recognized who he was and kissed his feet with all the reverence due to such a personage. He was warmly thanked, and was granted titles and indulgences, which have been retained to this day by the lord canons and the church of Compostella.

We returned to the inn, where we passed another cheerful evening. Early next morning we deposited our belongings with Sig. Ercole, for we fancied the idea of going to Santa Maria de Finisterre. I shall describe the journey briefly, so that any other pilgrim who wishes to go may know the road. We left by way of the gate on the south side of the city,[d] passing a few barren hills until we reached a place called Puente Maceira, a distance of three leagues. From here we came to another small town called Cegua, then Allas Barreres, one league, and Bon Jesús, two leagues. From here to Puente Oliveira it is two leagues. Next comes another little village called Cée, two leagues, and from there to Finisterre, another two.

14
THE SUNSET LAND
Finisterre

A *The beacon was presumably to warn local people about unwelcome visitors – see below.*

Fig. 82 *The west front of the church of Santa Maria de Finisterre. The free-standing arcade once formed a vestibule, or narthex, of the church itself.*

SANTA MARIA FINISTERRE IS A VERY SMALL church. It has a sacred image of the Blessed Virgin and a miraculous crucifix, life size, covered with relief carving. The church stands at the very edge of the land. This is a promontory, or rather I should say the tip of a hill which runs westward to the ocean. At the end of the promontory, near the water, stands this little church with the two sacred images: the Blessed Virgin and a crucifix. On the summit of the promontory is a tower, or rather a lantern, which they call in their language a *farol*. This tower is there so that a beacon can be lit on top of it at night, or during the day if necessary. The reason is that all the nations that sail on the ocean, whether to the north, the west the east or the south, can recognize this cape, or promontory.[a] They often disembark here, particularly those unbelievers who inhabit the northern kingdoms, also those from the west and south, that is from America, the largest of the four parts of the world; not to mention the ones from Africa, in the south, and those from Asia in the east. As I said, they all come in to land here and disembark, causing much trouble to the inhabitants of these shores.

But the sacred image of Mary and the one of her most beloved Son are pledged to defend this place against such rabble. Among the miracles they have wrought is the following: a Moorish vessel once put in here, whereupon the Moors immediately rushed to the church. When they saw the crucifix they attacked and insulted it. One of them very rashly drew his scimitar and raised his arm to strike it. But on doing so his arm became suspended motionless in the air, like a statue. His companions witnessed the miracle, while he, becoming aware of the offence, prayed to Christ to forgive him, promising he would become a Christian. He

Before the discovery of America Cape Finisterre was the western tip of the known world, literally the 'land's end.' In ancient myths it was the sunset region, associated with death and the after-life. Near the lighthouse there was said to be a large rectangular rock carved out with a shallow representation of the human form. It was a Celtic 'altar of the sun' on which sacrifice was made at sunset. Its where-abouts is unknown, if it ever ex-isted. The church of Santa Maria was founded in the 12th century. The two images Laffi mentions are still there. The Virgin is the work of Francisco de Anta, done in 1640. The crucifix resembles the crucifix of Burgos and is probably about the same date, 13th century. According to legend it miracu-lously floated ashore, but whence it came no one knew.

returned his scimitar to the scabbard and went with all his companions to the nearby town called Cée; there they were baptised and then continued on their journey.[a]

Santa Maria Finisterre has been well built and fortified to defend itself against the raids of these barbarians. Many

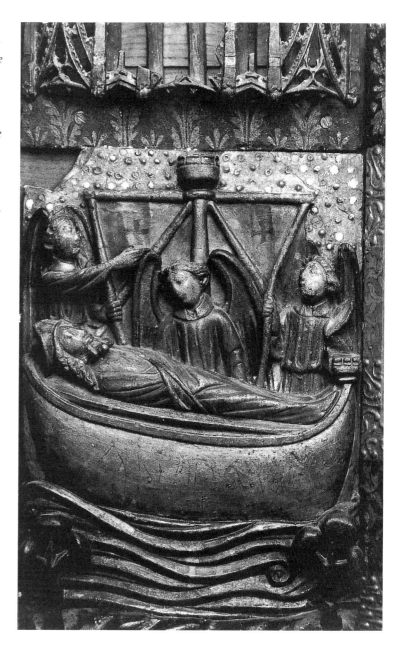

Fig. 83 *The body of St James transported to Spain. English alabaster, 15th century. (Reliquary chapel, Compos-tella cathedral.)*

B *There is an old saying, 'Quien va a Santiago e non va al Padrón, o faz romería o non', which roughly means, 'he who goes to Santiago and goes not to Padrón, has either completed his pilgrimage or he has not.' It was incumbent on every pilgrim to continue onwards as far as Padrón for the reason Laffi gives.*

The account of St James's martyrdom, how his disciples brought his body by sea to Padrón and carried it thence to Compostella is first told in a document that dates between about 1106 and 1139. Later versions embroidered it with other miraculous elements. Scholars today regard the story as having no historical substance. The origin of the cult of St James in Spain, which existed, at least in the south, in the early 7th century, has to be sought elsewhere. His supposed tomb was discovered in the first half of the 9th century (see Fletcher, R.A., Saint James's Catapult: the Life and Times of Diego Gelmirez, *Oxford, 1984 especially chap. 3 and app. A). Legend also maintained that when the disciples took the body out of the boat at the end of their journey they laid it on a rock which became soft to receive the sacred burden. Some scholars maintain that the various legends concerning St James in this coastal region were created by the early medieval Church to help them establish Christian worship in place of the older pagan rites (see Murguía, Manuel, 'Galicia', in* España, sus monumentos y artes, su naturaleza e historia, *Barcelona, 1981, pp.131-7).*

people have come to live here, maintaining a guard so that pilgrims and other folk can travel about in safety. If any of the heathens' vessels land here they immediately light a fire on the tower which, as I said, stands at the top of the promontory. This is a signal to neighbouring places, which in turn pass on a similar signal. Within an hour the whole kingdom of Galicia is warned of the danger. The men all arm themselves and go straight off to defend themselves against the common foe.

In the church there are many memorials to famous people who came here. On the way back you can, should you wish, go as we did by way of Iria Flavia, a town half a day's journey from Compostella which has a fine seaport. It is now called Padrón, and lies further south along the coast. This is the town and port where the body of St James the apostle landed when it was transported from Jerusalem to Spain. The port has one very wondrous thing: a ship of ordinary size, all of white marble. A hundred pair of oxen could not move it, still less a man. Yet a man can turn it with a single finger any way he wishes, though if he uses his whole strength, with both hands, he cannot move it. They told us that this was the ship which brought the body of St James from Jerusalem to Galicia, and that as soon as his disciples had taken the sacred body off the ship it turned into marble. Thus it could not be used by anyone and could not be taken away. It is always covered by the water, and can be seen only when the sea recedes in its ebb and flow. We were told about this by a number of Spaniards who took us round the town to show us the most interesting sights.[b]

When we left Iria Flavia, we returned to Compostella and went to see Sig. Ercole Zani, who was overjoyed that we had returned safely. We rested for a few hours, and then walked round the town, getting one or two things. After that we picked up our belongings and went to St James. We said our final prayers, and left the church. At the doorway of the archbishop's palace, which is near the doorway of the church to the north, we saw a large group of people with some decorum in their step, as if in a religious procession. We stopped to watch, and saw that it was a procession of priests, friars and canons of St James, walking two by two towards the church. After them came a man wearing a long and very old-fashioned sleeveless robe, with a cap on his head like a priest's biretta, topped by a most magnificent tassel in two colours, white and blue. It hung down on all sides, almost covering the whole of the biretta. We asked what this was about, and were told that he was a gentleman who had just received his doctorate.[a] They were going to St James to offer their thanks to him.

We then went back to our inn and, after taking farewell of our host and a number of friends who had been our companions, we left Compostella in the name of God and St James on the 3rd of July 1670 to return home.[b]

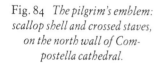

Fig. 84 *The pilgrim's emblem: scallop shell and crossed staves, on the north wall of Compostella cathedral.*

Appendix

LAFFI'S TIMETABLE

By James Hogarth

L AFFI IS PRECISE ABOUT THE DATE OF HIS departure from Bologna (16th April 1670) and the beginning of his return journey from Compostella (3rd July) – though I think there is some doubt about the latter date. There are a number of other key dates between these termini. Laffi was in Turin for the festival of the Holy Shroud on 4th May; he was in Castelnaudary on Pentecost (Sunday 25th May in 1670); he was in Orthez for Corpus Christi (Thursday 5th June in 1670); he was in Logroño on the feast of St Anthony of Padua (13th June); he was in Rabanal on the feast of John the Baptist (24th June); and he was in Compostella on the feast of the Visitation (2nd July).

It is possible to match these dates fairly closely to Laffi's narration. This close fit strengthens confidence in the reliability of his account – and evokes admiration of his walking ability.

I append a sketch of the complete timetable. The place opposite each date is the place where Laffi spent the night on that date. Overnight stops for which there is no firm evidence – suggested either to avoid an unrealistically long stage or sometimes to make up the right number of days between key dates – are shown between square brackets. The eight key dates are shown in the right column. Distances are approximate.

The least satisfactory bit of the timetable is the Italian section, where Laffi records few overnight stops and is vague about how many days he spent in Milan. The stopovers suggested are purely speculative. From Novara onwards it is possible to identify almost all the points at which he stopped for the night, though a few of them cannot be exactly located on the map. Between two key dates which are close together the intervening stages can be exactly dated;

elsewhere they may be a day adrift, making it necessary to postulate an unrecorded overnight stop. And in Compostella itself the programme cannot be reconciled with a departure date on 3rd July. The earliest I can make it is the 5th, and then only by assuming, without evidence, that the procession of the Visitation was on the vigil of the feast.

Remarks	DATE	PLACE	DISTANCE[a]	KEY DATES
A *Distances below are in km.*	APRIL			
	16	[Modena]	39	*Departure from Bologna*
	17	[Reggio]	20	
	18	[Parma]	27	
	19	?		
B *From Parma.*	Sun. 20	[Piacenza]	48[b]	
	21	[Lodi]	29	
	22	[Melegnano]		
C *From Lodi.*	23-27	Milan	31[c]	
	28	[Boffalora]		
	29	Novara		
D *From Milan.*	30	[Vercelli]	74[d]	
	MAY			
	1	San Germano		
E *From Vercelli.*	2	Chivasso	46[e]	
	3	Turin	26	
	Sun. 4	Santo Ambrogio		*Festival of the Holy Shroud*
F *From Turin.*	5	[Susa]	53[f]	
	6	Oulx	28	
	7	Briançon	35	
	8	Châteauroux	42	
	9	St-Étienne-le-Laus	41	
	10	Lazer	40	
	Sun. 11	Séderon	49	
	12	Mormoiron	57	
	13-14	Avignon	36	
G *Not located on the map.*	15	St-Étienne[g]	20	
	16	Milhaud	30	
	17	Montpellier	55	
H *Not located on the map.*	Sun. 18	Ruvirum[h]	30	
	19	Béziers	40	
	20	Narbonne	23	
	21	Lézignan	21	
	22	Carcassonne	34	
I *Extra day unaccounted for.*	23	?[i]		
	24	Castelnaudary	37	

LAFFI'S TIMETABLE

Remarks	DATE	PLACE	DISTANCE	KEY DATES
	Sun. 25	Baziège	38	Pentecost
	26-27	Toulouse	23	
	28	Gimont	54	
	29	Auch	24	
	30	Montesquiou	29	
	31	Marciac	20	
	JUNE			
J *Between Maubourguet and Anoye.*	Sun. 1	?^{j}		
K *From Marciac.*	2	Morlaàs	42^k	
L *Beyond Lescar.*	3	?^{l}		
M *From Morlaàs.*	4	Orthez	50^m	
	5	Sauveterre	20	Corpus Christi
N *Beyond St-Jean-Pied-de-Port.*	6	?^{n}		
O *From Sauveterre.*	7-8	Roncesvalles	70°	
	9	Pamplona	43	
	10	Puente la Reina	23	
	11	Los Arcos	39	
	12	Logroño	25	
	13	Nájera	26	Feast of St Anthony of Padua
P *Laffi notes that it is Saturday.*	14	Grañón	24^p	
Q *Near San Juan de Ortega.*	Sun. 15	Villanueva^q	40	
	16	Burgos	21	
	17	Hontanas	30	
	18	Frómista	31	
	19	Calzadilla/Cueza	36	
	20	Burgo Ranero	38	
	21	León	35	
	Sun. 22	Puente de Orbigo	30	
	23	Rabanal	35	
	24	Ponferrada	29	Feast of John the Baptist
	25	Villafranca/Bierzo	21	
R *Beyond Herrerias.*	26	?^{r}	21	
S *Suggested to avoid too long a stage.*	27	[Triacastela]^s	27	
	28	Puertomarin	35	
	Sun. 29	Mellid	37	
	30	Santiago	50	
	JULY			
T *Procession on Vigil of Visitation?*	1	Santiago		?^{t}
	2	Santiago		Feast of Visitation
	3	Santiago		
U *To Finisterre and back to Santiago?*	4	Santiago?^{u}		
	5			Departure from Santiago?